Rosemary Hemphill is an expert on the history and cultivation of herbs, and in this *Herb Collection* she shares with others her knowledge of these varied and lovely plants. She has collected here the most delectable of her recipes, as well as ideas for gifts such as aromatic bath sachets, clove oranges, scented note-paper, and other pretty conceits.

A completely revised and metricated edition of her *Fragrance and Flavour, Rosemary Hemphill's Herb Collection* is a treasury of information, and as helpful in practical ways as it is charming in appearance.

A companion volume, *Rosemary Hemphill's Spice Collection,* is also available.

What reviewers said about *Fragrance and Flavour:*
"A delightful book which combines recipes with gossip, information about the growing and use of a couple of dozen herbs."

Sydney Morning Herald

"Charmingly presented, her book is a delight to read, quite apart from its usefulness."

Times Literary Supplement (London)

Also by Rosemary Hemphill
Spice and Savour
Herbs for all Seasons
Cooking with Herbs and Spices
Rosemary Hemphill's Spice Collection

AN ANGUS & ROBERTSON BOOK

First published in Australia by Angus & Robertson Publishers in 1959
First published in the United Kingdom by Angus & Robertson (UK) in 1959
Reprinted in 1961, 1965, 1966, 1969, 1973, 1979, 1982, 1984
Revised edition 1989
This edition published by Collins/Angus & Robertson
Publishers Australia in 1990

Collins/Angus & Robertson Publishers Australia
Unit 4, Eden Park, 31 Waterloo Road, North Ryde
NSW 2113, Australia

William Collins Publishers Ltd
31 View Road, Glenfield, Auckland 10, New Zealand

Angus & Robertson (UK)
16 Golden Square, London W1R 4BN, United Kingdom

Copyright © Rosemary Hemphill 1964, 1989

National Library of Australia
Cataloguing-in-publication data:

Hemphill, Rosemary, 1922–
  Rosemary Hemphill's herb collection.

  Includes index.
  ISBN 0 207 16143 7.

  1. Cookery (Herbs). 2. Herbs. I. Title.
  II. Title: Herb collection. III. Title: Fragrance and flavour:
  the growing and use of herbs.

641.6'57

Typeset in 11pt Garamond 3 by Best-set Typesetter Ltd
Printed in Singapore

16 15 14 13 12 11
95 94 93 92 91 90

ROSEMARY HEMPHILL'S

HERB
COLLECTION

ANGUS
& ROBERTSON

for
John

My sincere thanks are due to my mother
for drawing on her knowledge of English
literature, and to my husband for his cheerful
and unselfish attitude when meals were
late and often experimental.

ACKNOWLEDGMENTS

The publishers acknowledge with thanks the permission of the copyright owners to reprint the poems "The Sunken Garden", by Walter de la Mare, and "The Clove Orange", by Eleanor Farjeon.

Contents

FRAGRANCE & FLAVOUR
Introduction
· 1 ·

GROWING & HARVESTING
· 9 ·

GROWING HERBS INDOORS
· 15 ·

FRAGRANT GIFTS
· 19 ·

HERBS
· 25 ·

Angelica · 27

Balm · 29

Basil · 32

Bay Leaves · 35

Bergamot · 37

Borage · 40

Chervil · 42

Chicory · 45

Chives · 46

Coriander · 49

Dill · 51

Fennel · 54

Garlic · 56

Lavender · 59

Marjoram · 63

Mint · 67

Oregano · 71

Parsley · 74

Rosemary · 76

Roses · 79

Sage · 84

Savory · 87

Scented-leaved
geraniums · 89

Tarragon · 94

Thyme · 97

HERBAL TEAS
· 103 ·

INDEX
· 109 ·

This metric conversion table is included for the convenience of our readers. The equivalents in it are not exact—500 g is slightly more than 1 lb, for example. But this does not matter so long as you follow *either* the metric weights and measures *or* the imperial in the recipe. Never use a mixture of the two, as the recipe proportions will then be slightly altered. *Note*: A dessertspoon is equivalent to 2 metric teaspoons.

Weights

Ounces/Pounds	Grams
1 ounce	30 g
4 ounces (¼ lb)	125 g
8 ounces (½ lb)	250 g
12 ounces (¾ lb)	375 g
16 ounces (1 lb)	500 g
24 ounces (1½ lb)	750 g
32 ounces (2 lb)	1000 g (1 kg)

Measures

Pints	Millilitres
¼ pint	150 ml
½ pint	300 ml
¾ pint	450 ml
1 pint	600 ml

Temperatures

Fahrenheit (°F)	Celsius (°C)
250	120
300	150
350	175
400	200
425	220
475	245

I know a bank whereon the wild thyme blows,
Where oxlips and the nodding violet grows
Quite over-canopied with luscious woodbine,
With sweet musk-roses, and with eglantine...
            A Midsummer Night's Dream. OBERON, ACT II, SCENE I.

It is in the planning and planting of gardens that many people express their sense of the beautiful and find contentment. To some it may be the simple joy of stepping on to a peppermint-scented carpet of pennyroyal in the early morning; to others the pleasure of seeing the jewelled flowers of a favourite tea-tree glistening through the mistiness of a spider's web.

Originally man depended on plants for food and medicine, and many of the ornamental flowers, shrubs and trees that are part of the garden landscape today, were once valued for their healing properties as well as for their beauty. All through history there have been stories of gardens—from the splendour of the Hanging Gardens of Babylon, one of the seven wonders of the ancient world, to the monastic "physic gardens" of medieval days, where monks grew herbs and concocted them into healing potions and salves for the sick.

There is an interesting biblical tale, nearly 2000 years old, told in *The Bible as History*, of the herbal gardens of the village of Mataria, near Cairo— the Queen of Sheba is said to have taken seeds of balsam as a present to King Solomon, and scented bushes from the seeds grew in Jericho. Many years later Cleopatra took cuttings of these valuable plants to Mataria. Later still, during their flight into Egypt, Joseph, Mary, and Jesus took refuge in these fragrant balsam gardens of Mataria.

It is said that in ancient Egypt the homes of the nobles on the river Nile had cool gardens within the courtyards, the floors of which, unearthed centuries later by excavators, were exquisitely tiled by craftsmen to show flowers, grasses and birds. The love of gardens has stayed in us and today we have landscape windows, and doors opening on to vine-covered terraces, bringing "the outdoors in" for a restful and harmonious atmosphere.

The garden where scented plants grow has a strong attraction, particularly for the winged creatures that bring life to any garden. Bees, especially, love bergamot or bee-balm, and borage too, which is, incidentally, often grown as a crop for bees; buddleia, with its trusses of soft, purple flower-heads similar to lilac blossom, brings flocks of butterflies, and if there are a few berry trees and a trough of water in the garden, birds will be found there chattering and splashing and appreciating it all.

My grandfather always thought of the birds in his garden in Kent. There were bird-baths, and bird-tables for crumbs and seed, carefully placed over the four acres of his garden, and in winter there were lumps of suet in halved coconuts hanging from the trees to nourish the birds when times were lean during the cold weather. This was the garden, "New Farm", mentioned in the *Memoirs of Lady Hester Stanhope*, to which Lady Hester, William Pitt's niece, used to ride over to admire the yew trees. The trees are no longer there, the garden now being only a memory, with rows of houses standing in its place.

For the sake of Shakespeare's lines sung by Oberon, it would be fitting to add to a scented garden the age-old enchantment of honey-laden thyme; oxlips (*Primula elatior*) one of the primrose family; "the nodding violet" with its fresh, sweet scent; "luscious woodbine", which is honeysuckle; eglantine, the sweet briar rose and the musk rose (*Rosa moschata*). Eleanour Sinclair Rohde, the English authority and writer on herbs, says: "The true musk rose has single white blooms borne in large trusses. . . .*R. moschata* is also a parent, or rather, grandparent, of such famous roses as Cloth of Gold."

A scented garden is not complete without a variety of herbs, and they are very interesting to grow. Each plant has its own characteristic flavour and scent, which may be utilized in cooking, in making fragrant and beneficial "tisanes" (nourishing decoctions) or gathering and drying for pot-pourri or sweet sachets. Every herb has its own legend too, and it is almost worth growing them for this alone.

Although herbs may grow among all the other plants in the garden, it is more satisfactory to have them together—you are not then wondering if the thyme is hiding under the jasmine, or if you will have to disturb the columbines to find the chives! When the herbs are growing together it is an easy matter to survey them at a glance and decide which ones you would like to pick and put in sandwiches, or in a rice salad, or use in other ways.

Herb sandwiches have a fresh and pleasing flavour—everyone likes them. Spread slices of brown bread—brown seems to go best with herbs—with butter and a little cream cheese or marmite, fill with chopped herbs and cut off the crusts. Almost any herbs will do, although it is wise to use a little discretion; for instance, marjoram and basil are pungent and go well with chives or parsley. Pennyroyal, which has a strong flavour of peppermint, is best mixed with parsley and a leaf or two of eau-de-Cologne mint; mustard and cress are old favourites, and on very hot days spearmint sandwiches are refreshing.

In the early morning and in the evening, when there are shadows and the light is soft, I am reminded of Walter de la Mare's poem, "The Sunken Garden",

> *Speak not ——— whisper not;*
> *Here bloweth thyme and bergamot;*
> *Softly on the evening hour,*
> *Secret herbs their spices shower.*
> *Dark-spiked rosemary and myrrh,*
> *Lean-stalked, purple lavender;*
> *Hides within her bosom, too,*
> *All her sorrows, bitter rue.*
>
> *Breathe not ——— trespass not;*
> *Of this green and darkling spot,*

Latticed from the moon's beams,
Perchance a distant dreamer dreams;
Perchance upon its darkening air,
The unseen ghosts of children fare,
Faintly swinging, sway and sweep,
Like lovely sea-flowers in the deep;
While, unmoved, to watch and ward,
Amid its gloomed and daisied sward,
Stands with bowed and dewy head
That one little leaden Lad.

It is possible for everyone to grow herbs, whether their garden is large or small, or even if they have no garden. People living in flats may grow many herbs successfully in suitable containers; details of how this may be achieved are given in the chapter Growing Herbs Indoors.

Nearly all herbs prefer light, well-drained soil and plenty of sunlight so that they may produce their essential oils. The few that prefer shade and a moist position, such as angelica, bergamot and chervil may be planted in the shadiest corner, perhaps under a lemon-scented verbena tree, and given the water they require.

A sunny pathway planting of herbs within easy reach of the kitchen has endless possibilities, and a sundial set at a pleasing angle gives interest. Sundials for the southern hemisphere are available. A base may be made of stones cemented together, or an old tree stump of the right size is quite effective.

A wheel-garden or a ladder-garden makes compact plantings. For a wheel-garden, lay an old cartwheel on prepared ground, and plant the herbs between the spokes with either a sundial or a tall, bushy perennial, such as rosemary, wormwood, sage or lavender in the middle. Graduate the size of the other herbs as they radiate from the centre, with the low border plants, chives, parsley, pennyroyal and thyme for instance, at the edges. For a ladder-garden, lay the ladder along the ground, and plant herbs between the rungs.

For a larger garden, a corner might be found for a properly enclosed herb garden laid out with geometrical beds. These gardens may vary in size and shape from perhaps a square garden 3 metres by 3 metres (10 feet by 10 feet) to a rectangular garden 5 metres by 8 metres (18 feet by 25 feet) or larger. It is a matter of taste and room. There are various ways of enclosing a garden like this; for a formal effect a low hedge of clipped dwarf box (*Buxus semper-virens*) is traditional, neat and attractive. A scented hedge of either French lavender, hyssop, "lad's love" (*Artemisia abrotanum*), winter savory or rose-mary is equally as good. The garden may also be enclosed with crossed sap-lings for climbing roses to grow over, or a low picket fence, painted white. Brick or stone is used, too, and even though this takes more time to con-struct it is very attractive when completed.

For those who may wish to attempt a garden of this kind, the following description of a typical one will serve as a guide. An area 8 metres by 5 metres (25 feet by 18 feet) was pegged out and surrounded with a wall, 1 metre (3 feet) high, of "ballast" stone. The stones were cemented together, not too neatly, so as to give them a rough, weathered look. The wall was made double, with a space in the middle about 30 centimetres (12 inches) wide to contain soil for plants to grow in. Holes were left in the cement for drainage.

In the middle of the garden there is a sundial, with simple geometrical beds of herbs and stone paths radiating from it. There is also a stone seat, with English lavender growing on either side of it. The same sweet-smelling plant borders the pathway leading from the herb garden into the rose garden.

With a garden of this type, shrubs and plants of varying heights may be grown from the top of the wall very effectively. Sturdy French lavender, pros-trate rosemary, creeping thymes, wormwood, lavender-cotton and the old, scented wallflower are just a few that are suitable.

Whatever the size of your herb patch, it will give you joy, and if you have not grown herbs before, there is a new adventure in fragrance and flavour waiting for you.

GROWING
and
·HARVESTING·

When planning to grow herbs, have the position and ground ready in time for planting in spring. A sunny aspect and light soil is a good all-round rule for growing herbs. A few such as chervil, bergamot and angelica prefer semi-shade, and this may be arranged by choosing the most protected position for them.

Sow the seeds in seed boxes after the frosts are over, and, when big enough to handle, plant the seedlings out. If well cared for they will grow rapidly and be ready to start using within a few weeks. Water them in dry weather and keep them weeded and cultivated.

Herbs respond to constant picking: chives become sturdier and send out fresh, tender leaves more quickly; parsley and chervil leaves should be picked from the outside always, allowing the new leaves to grow from the middle; basil must have the tops continually picked out to make a sturdy bush and to prevent it from flowering too soon.

The low-growing herbs best suited for edging are pennyroyal, chives, fragrant thyme, chervil, variegated balm and hyssop. Herbs of medium height are spicy tarragon, coriander, bush basil, oregano, winter savory, mint, marjoram, lemon balm and chamomile. The taller herbs to use for background planting or to feature as a central point are angelica, lovage, sweet basil, dill, fennel, sage, lavender, rosemary, rue, anchusa and chicory. Bergamot must be cherished in a sheltered, rather moist position. Mint and tarragon must have room to spread, so it is wise to remember this when planting. Borage is lovely if left to itself and allowed to grow in a misty blue drift in a corner on its own.

The perfumed herbs should be grown for making into scented gifts, or to pick for fragrant posies or "tussie-mussies" as they were once called.

Many of them are used to impart their aroma to certain food. There are the lavenders—English (*Lavandula vera*) and French (*L. dentata* and *L. stoechas*), to name but three varieties. Rosemary is used sparingly in cooking veal and pork dishes, but it is more often grown for its sweet scent and meaning of friendship and remembrance. Rue is the "herb of grace" and should be near-by, for "where there's rosemary there's rue". A small amount of the chopped leaves is often used in vegetable cocktails.

Scented-leaved geraniums are also used in flavouring some foods, but are better known for the fragrance of their leaves. Lemon-scented verbena grows into a graceful tree with deliciously perfumed leaves which retain their lemon scent long after they have been dried and are brittle with age; a few fresh leaves impart a delicate flavour when baking milk puddings. Heliotrope or "cherry pie" is a soft cloud of mauve when in full bloom and is one of the most fragrant herbs; grow it in a sheltered sunny position.

Wallflowers, the old yellow and tawny ones, contain in the flowers the distilled essence of all the mellow summer scents, warm walls, new-mown hay and the sweetness of all flowers; this plant was once a healing herb. Added to the few which have been mentioned are other well-known plants which were once valuable herbs—roses, violets, jasmine, primroses, clove-pinks, hollyhocks, foxglove and honeysuckle, all of which would be in keep-ing in a herb garden.

Have you ever thought of having a herb lawn, or a pathway made en-tirely of herbs? Thyme, pennyroyal and chamomile are all suitable for this. The hardy *Thymus serpyllum*, if given a chance to establish itself, makes a fragrant carpet. It cannot bear much traffic, so it would have to be grown in a special corner of its own. Thyme, grown over a mound of earth, makes a soft and scented seat; plant established roots, lift apart in the early spring and keep weed-free and well-watered.

Pennyroyal spreads very quickly, is extremely hardy, and discourages weeds once it has formed a thick mat. The fresh peppermint scent is released when trodden on, and it would be a pity to mow it in the spring when its small spires of lavender-coloured flowers are in bloom making a "fairy mead". Plant roots a metre (3 feet) apart in the spring and autumn. However, cut off the flowers when they fade to keep plants growing strongly.

Of English chamomile (*Anthemis nobilis*) E. S. Rohde says: "I wonder how many of the people who attend the royal garden parties at Buckingham Palace realize that big stretches of one of the lawns are planted with camomile?" It makes an excellent lawn and needs semi-shade and constant watering in dry weather. Put in the plants 10 centimetres (4 inches) apart in spring or autumn. These carpeting herbs may be placed between stones or bricks for pathways in the herb garden.

As the season advances and the herbs approach maturity it is time to decide those to dry for winter use. Although leaves of marjoram, thyme and oregano are always available, they are even more pungent when dried, and now is the time, while the atmosphere is dry, to do it. Herbs should be harvested just before the buds open into full flower for the greatest flavour and abundance of natural oils.

Gather them in dry weather, after the dew has left them and before the hot sun has drawn out the natural oils, hang them up to dry in bundles in an airy passageway, or lay them on paper in a dark cupboard. Oven-drying is not good unless wet weather makes it necessary, as much of the flavour is lost in this way. The drying time varies from about twelve days to three weeks. When dry, strip the leaves from the stalks on to clean paper and pour them into clean, dry, airtight jars which have been clearly labelled. Keep the herbs separate so that blending becomes a personal choice. It is interesting to experiment with flavours.

With the coming of autumn in the herb garden, the flowers which have been left to bear next season's crop of herbs must be gathered when the seeds are ripe. Put the seeds away in labelled airtight envelopes or little jars. Cut out dead stalks in the garden and trim the plants.

When winter comes sweet basil will be missed, but instead there are fresh marjoram leaves which are very aromatic and pungent and seem to suit the season; winter vegetables after all have stronger flavours.

By mid-winter the herb garden will be lying dormant, waiting for spring, and as many of the herbs are perennials, their second year will be worth seeing. It is a good idea at this time to give the ground a light top-dressing of well-decayed poultry humus.

When spring comes again and the garden is established, it is time to think of the other aspects connected with herb gardening. The sweet-smelling herbs, flowers and fruit needed for making pot-pourri, lavender bags, sachets, pomander oranges or apples, herb pillows, scented coat-hangers and perfumed rubbing lotions are ready. These make delightful and unusual gifts at Christmas.

Kind thoughts surround sweet smelling things, and it is pleasant to carry on this old tradition.

GROWING HERBS
· INDOORS ·

People who live in flats and would like to grow herbs may do so successfully if a few simple rules are followed. First of all the right soil mixture is important, and it should consist of sand, leaf-mould and soil in equal parts. Nurseries sometimes sell this mixture in polythene bags. Secondly, herbs love sunlight so at some stage during the day it is desirable for them to bask in it, particularly by an open window. The third point to remember is to keep them watered—once a day should be sufficient. About once a fortnight add a little liquid fertilizer, which is obtainable at most nurseries, to the watering can.

When planting, cover the hole in the container with a few pieces of broken crock or some stones, and then fill with soil. Put in the seedlings, firming them well with the hands, and water well.

Nearly all herbs will grow in containers, the taller-growing varieties such as Florence fennel, borage and sage becoming satisfactorily dwarfed with the confined root-space. The herbs of low and medium growth, bush basil, chervil, chives, marjoram, parsley, and thyme are all excellent for this purpose. Herbs with rampant root systems, for instance balm, winter savory, the mints, oregano, pennyroyal and tarragon should be put severely on their own, or they will choke out the others. Lavender, rosemary, and the scented-leaved geraniums will not attain the height they would reach if growing in the garden, but if repotted every year with new soil, and when necessary given a larger container, they will give pleasure for a very long time. Angelica, chicory and lovage grow too high to be considered.

There are various containers on the marker suitable for growing herbs in, and, starting from the kitchen, here are a few suggestions: pots of terra-cotta or china grouped on kitchen window ledges are excellent and may be moved about for convenience; let the mint run riot in a squat fifteen centimetre (six inch) azalea pot; a trough of tin, cement or terra-cotta on the window-sill with several herbs grouped together, is convenient, a good combination being marjoram, chives and parsley, although this is really a matter of personal choice. A graceful, small wrought-iron stand filled with herbs in pots, or a trough fitted snugly into it, may be used either on a kitchen window-sill or as a centrepiece on the dining-room table. It is delightful to look at and amusing to snip off the leaves to flavour a French salad to be mixed at the table.

As wrought iron is light and airy it is particularly suitable for flats, whether large or small, blending with any type of furniture and all styles of decoration.

For balconies, roof gardens, back doors or where space is otherwise restricted, a large "strawberry pot" with from six to nine pockets is a good idea. The procedure for filling this container is to prepare the soil and put in the plants as the pot is filled with earth, leaving the most decorative herb until last for the top. The soil may be bought ready mixed, or it may be prepared by mixing equal quantities of sand, leaf-mould and soil. With this light soil, water reaches every herb, right down to the bottom. Experiments have shown that a heavier soil combination is a failure. The sand is necessary to prevent the soil from clogging, and the leaf-mould is important for airiness and fertilizing, and as mentioned earlier, this mixture is excellent for other types of containers also.

Let imagination help you in deciding the containers and stands to use. Secondhand or antique shops are a treasure-trove to discerning eyes. With a little paint or polish the most unlikely article may turn out to be an original and striking holder.

· FRAGRANT GIFTS ·

Imagination, and willing fingers, which need not be too nimble, are the main requirements for making many useful and acceptable gifts which originate from the garden.

Thought and care are important in making the article look attractive. Time is another factor; pot-pourri takes time to mature, pomander balls are a little slow but not difficult to make, and, of course, it is necessary to wait for the lavender to dry before putting it into sachets. A scented gift has the quality of conveying the personality of the giver much more than any other present. A pot-pourri can be a very memorable gift, and one that will stir grateful memories in the receiver. Even during the warmest summer day it will scent a room with fresh perfume, and the hotter the day the more scent it will release. The lid must be replaced at night, and the dried fragrant leaves and flowers stirred frequently.

Fragrant powdered orris root is a necessary ingredient in many of the following recipes and it is interesting to know that it comes from the dried root of the white-flowering Florentine iris, *Iris florentina*. And now for a few gift suggestions.

A · Pomander · Ball · or · Clove Orange · or · Apple

It is important to select a ripe, fresh thin-skinned orange. Stick it full of cloves, starting from the stalk-end and going round the orange until it is covered, roll it well in a teaspoonful of orris powder and a teaspoonful of cinnamon mixed together, pressing the powder well in. Wrap the orange in tissue paper and put it away in a dark cupboard for a week or two. Press a staple into the top of the orange and tie a small bow to it, or thread a length of narrow ribbon through the staple so that the pomander may hang from a coathanger in a wardrobe. Corded ribbon in muted shades of either gold, rose, soft blue, lavender or sage green looks particularly attractive with the snuff-brown of the pomander and its old-world appearance.

A clove orange serves two purposes: it helps to keep moths away from drawers, cupboards and linen closets, as well as scenting them. One hung from the china door-knob of a sitting room can look charming. The orange becomes "petrified" and does not decay in any way—it just grows smaller and smaller. Sometimes pomanders ten years old may be seen, still spicily fragrant, as hard as iron, and very, very small. Fresh apples are made in the same way.

Here is a delightful poem called "The Clove Orange" by Eleanor Farjeon:

> *I'll make a clove orange to give to my darling,*
> *I'll make a clove orange to please my delight,*
> *And lay in her coffer to sweeten her linen*
> *And hang by her pillow to sweeten her night.*
>
> *I'll choose a small orange as round as the moon is,*
> *That ripened its cheek in the sunniest grove,*
> *And when it is dry as a midsummer hayfield*
> *I'll stick it all round with the head of a clove.*
>
> *To spice the dull sermon in church of a Sunday,*
> *Her orange of cloves in her bag she shall take;*
> *When parson is prosy and eyelids are drowsy,*
> *One sniff at her spice-ball will charm her awake.*
>
> *And when she walks forth in the highways and byways*
> *Where fevers are prone and infection is rife,*
> *On her palm she shall carry her little clove orange,*
> *A charm against sickness, to guard her sweet life.*
>
> *And moth shall not haunt her most delicate garment,*
> *Nor spectre her delicate dream in the night,*
> *When she hangs in her chamber her little dried orange.*
> *I've studded with cloves to delight my Delight.*

Lavender · Bags

Many people today make fragrant lavender bags as gifts which are always welcome. For those who have never made them the following simple directions are given:

Pick English lavender heads just before they are in full bloom. Gather them when the dew has gone and before the hot sun has drawn the scent from the blossoms, spread them in a cool airy place to dry, never in direct sunlight because the sun's rays draw out much of the valuable aroma even when picked. When dry, rub the tiny flowers from the stalks and fill your lavender bags. If these are not ready, store the dried lavender in an air-tight jar. Lavender-coloured muslin or organdie are favourite materials to use for the bags which are usually drawn in near the top with lavender ribbon tied in a bow. A little silk embroidery enhances the appearance of the sachets. There is scope for the imagination in making lavender bags, and they need not be of the conventional materials and colours—new ideas are always refreshing.

Sweet · Bags

Sweet bags are similar to lavender bags. They are filled with a variety of ingredients, and while lavender bags are used for scenting drawers and linen cupboards, sweet bags may be used not only for this purpose, but for putting under pillows, and hanging on the backs of chairs, where the warmth and pressure from the head releases the perfume. How charmingly thoughtful our grandmothers were, and how unusual and pleasant it would be today for a guest in the spare-room to discover on retiring the fragrance of the sweet bag under her pillow.

The following recipes all are excellent for making sweet bags.

1. Dry equal quantities of lemon-scented geranium and rose-scented geranium leaves. Crumble and mix with the desired amount of dried lavender flowers and a little orris root powder. Fill pastel coloured silk bags.

2. Take 2 handfuls of dried rose petals, and add 60 g (2 oz) of orris root powder, a little common salt, 60 g (2 oz) of coriander seeds, 2 teaspoons of cinnamon, 1 teaspoon of ground cloves and 1 handful of dried orange blossom. Mix together and fill sachets.

3. Mix 2 handfuls each of dried wallflowers and rosemary flowers, 60 g (2 oz) of orris root powder, and 1 teaspoon of powdered nutmeg. Fill bags. This mixture is particularly aromatic and sweet. The rosemary flowers hold their perfume admirably and mingle well with the warm fragrance of wallflowers.

A · Scented · Coathanger

Make one of the preparations for a sweet sachet or lavender bag and fill a muslin bag the length of a wooden coathanger. Cover the hanger with plain material and sew the filled muslin bag into place on top of the hanger. Cover the hanger completely with a suitable material—silk, sprigged muslin, or organza in pastel colours are all pretty. Softly pleat the material and cover the hook too. An extra touch may be added by swinging a sweet sachet by a length of ribbon from the centre of the hanger.

Gift · Packages

A gift package of home-dried culinary herbs is a welcome present for a friend who is interested in cooking. Cover an old chocolate box or shoe box with pretty wallpaper, preferably one suited to this type of gift, patterned with leaves or flowers, and pack it with small airtight glass jars filled with separate herbs, carefully labelling each one. Paint a leaf or flower on the jar, too, if you wish; the manner in which each person expresses himself is individual and original. A gift package of the tea herbs may be prepared in the same way.

Rosemary · Rubbing · Lotion

Buy 600 ml (1 pint) of odourless rubbing alcohol from the chemist. Put crushed rosemary leaves and flowers, and the highly aromatic seeds, too, if you have them, into a jar. Pour the spirit over, cover and leave for two or three weeks, shaking occasionally. Strain and use. This makes a welcome gift for someone ill in bed. It has a much more pleasant smell than methylated spirit. If you cannot buy the alcohol, use white wine vinegar instead, the fragrant herbs cancel out the tang of vinegar. This recipe may be followed in the same way with other sweet-scented and pungent herbs and flowers, such as lavender, lemon verbena, balm, mint, rose petals, violets, carnations and scented-leaved geraniums.

Aromatics · for · the · Bath

Sprigs of rosemary are said to be invigorating additions to a bath. A gift package may be made in the way as described for culinary herbs. Fill small individual bags of plain coloured muslin with rosemary, pine needles, lavender heads, dried orange flowers and dried eau-de-Cologne mint, naming each herb on the muslin with a marking pencil; these bags are put into a hot bath and allowed to infuse.

Scented · Note-paper

Buy a box of white or pastel note-paper and envelopes and slip the sweet-bag mixture in small sachets between the layers of paper and envelopes. Re-wrap the box in cellophane with narrow ribbon finished with a sachet and ribbon-loops on the top. It does not take long for the perfume to permeate the paper.

Here are some old recipes from *The Scented Garden* by E. S. Rohde:

Honey · Soap

Take four ounces [125 g] of white soap and as much honey, half an ounce [15 g] of salt of tartar, and two or three drachms [10 ml] of the distilled Water of fumitory; mix the whole together. This soap cleanses the skin well, and renders it delicately white and smooth. It is also used advantageously to efface the marks of burns and scalds. ("The Toilet of Flora".)

Scented · Candles

Take Benjamin, storax, of each foure ounces [125 g], Frankincense, Olibanum, of each twelve ounces [375 g], Labdanum eighteen ounces [560 g], Nigella an ounce [30 g], Coriander seeds, Juniper berries, of each halfe an ounce [15 g]; liquid Storax sixe ounces [185 g], Turpentine halfe an ounce [15 g], forme them into Candles with gum: dragant and Rose water. (*The Charitable Physitian*, by Philibert Guibert, Physitian Regent in Paris, 1639.)

·HERBS·

*Their Tradition,
Culture, and Use*

The following chapter discusses twenty-five herbs suitable
for comestic conditions. Each entry includes something
of the herb's tradition, directions for cultivating it,
and recipes for its use.
The herbs are given in alphabetical order.

Angelica

As its name suggests, the perennial herb angelica (*Angelica archangelica*), has heavenly associations in ancient folklore. In her book *Herbs* and *Herb Gardening* E. S. Rohde says traditionally an angel revealed its qualities in a dream during a time of plague, and a piece of the root held in the mouth was commended to drive away the "pestilentiall aire".

It was very highly regarded in the old herb gardens, every part of the plant having some particular use. Today, oil distilled from the seeds and roots is used in flavouring liqueurs and wines and the leaves are used in making beneficial tisanes, and for flavouring stewed fruit. Candied angelica is well known, the stalk and leaf stems being used for this. Instructions for making angelica tea are given in the chapter Herbal Teas.

Angelica grows up to two metres (six feet) in height, and unlike most herbs prefers a moist, rich soil and shade. The seed will not germinate unless it is very fresh.

Glazed · Pears

4 large pears thoroughly dry	Angelica
1 cup passion-fruit pulp	1 teaspoon cinnamon or 4
1 cup water	coriander seeds
1/2 cup sugar	A little butter

Wash and core pears from the stalk end. In each hollow put a knob of butter, a little sugar and cinnamon, or 1 coriander seed. Place in a saucepan and pour over them a syrup made from the sugar and water boiled together for 10 minutes. Cover and simmer slowly until just tender, ladling the syrup over continually. Add the passion-fruit pulp.

Lift the pears out carefully and put on a dish. Pour the passion-fruit and syrup over the pears. Decorate each pear with a stalk of angelica. Chill, and serve with heavy cream.

Candied · Angelica

It is well worth while candying your own angelica; it is not much trouble, but takes a little time. If you plan ahead and quick results are not expected, then you are half way to having it done.

Select young stems and stalks of angelica. Cut into 12 cm (4 or 5 inch) lengths and place in a glass or crockery vessel, pour over them a boiling solution of 600 ml (1 pint) water and 125 g (1/4 lb) salt. Cover and leave for 24 hours. Lift out, drain on a wire drainer, peel and wash in cold water.

Make a syrup of 750 g (1 1/2 lb) sugar and 900 ml (1 1/2 pints) water, and boil for ten minutes. Place the angelica in the boiling syrup for 20 minutes; lift out and drain for 4 days on a wire drainer.

Reboil again for 20 minutes in the same syrup. Allow to cool in the syrup, lift out and drain for three or four days. Strew well with sugar and store in airtight jars.

Trifles and cakes are decorated with candied angelica cut into leaves, stems and fancy shapes, and that delightful Italian sweet cassata has angelica in it.

Stewed · Rhubarb · and · Angelica
Leaves

1 bunch rhubarb	*4 young angelica leaves*
1 cup water	*2 thin curls of lemon peel*
½ cup sugar	

Cut up rhubarb and put in saucepan with water, sugar, lemon peel and angelica leaves. Bring to boil and simmer until tender.

Serve chilled with whipped cream or yoghurt.

Balm

Balm (*Melissa officinalis*) is an easy perennial plant to grow. Like the mint family it prefers part shade and a moist position, and in the autumn it should be cut down to the ground. It has quite a rampant root system, but is easy to keep in check.

In spring the young lemon-scented leaves are fresh and attractive, and it grows rapidly into a thick and bushy plant nearly a metre (about three feet) high. In summer the series of small, white flowers carried on long stems are a great attraction to bees.

Balm was indispensable in the old herb garden. Refreshing teas and healing ointments were made from the leaves, and bee hives were often rubbed with it. The leaves are a valuable ingredient in pot-pourri too, the rather piercing lemon scent complementing some of the sweeter flower scents. A pot-pourri should be like well-cooked food that has many ingredients in its composition, the whole being a pleasing blend, but no one flavour or aroma being too predominant.

Balm, or lemon balm as it is sometimes called, dries well and retains its scent. A few dried leaves put in the teapot with your usual Indian tea makes an invigorating drink for fatigue, and in hot weather is refreshing.

Variegated balm (*M. officinalis variegata*) is grown more for its appearance than for practical purposes, although a leaf floated on top of an iced drink looks attractive. It is a perennial, of spreading habit, growing no more than thirty centimetres (twelve inches) high, and is most effective with its green and pale-gold foliage for rockeries, borders, and in flower arrangements too. It is very aromatic, the whole plant smelling of lemons. It must be watered in dry weather, and protected from too much frost.

The following recipes are for lemon balm, as it is hardier, but a few leaves of the variegated type are suitable for garnishing.

Balm · and · Marshmallow · Custard

600 ml (1 pint) milk	*1 vanilla bean*
2 eggs	*1 tablespoon fresh balm leaves,*
1 1/2 tablespoons sugar	*or 1 dessertspoon dried and*
6 marshmallows	*crumbled balm leaves*

Put the marshmallows in the bottom of a well-buttered fireproof dish. Whisk the eggs and sugar together, add milk, beat well and pour over the marshmallows. Put in the vanilla bean, and sprinkle the balm leaves on top. Place the dish in a shallow pan of cold water and bake slowly in a medium oven until set.

Serve chilled with cream—it seems to go particularly well with slices of fresh sugared pineapple.

Balm · and · Orange · Frosted
(A refreshing summer drink)

2 cups orange juice	*1 bunch balm leaves*
1 cup lemon juice	*1/2 cup sugar*
600 ml (1 pint) water	*Ice cubes*
2 bottles ginger ale	

Mix juices, balm leaves, sugar and water and chill overnight. Strain, add ginger ale just before serving and pour into glasses over cubes of ice. Float a balm leaf on the top of each drink.

The following salad is excellent with roast duck. It may also be served with turkey or ham.

Balm · Dressing · for · Orange · Salad

Peel 4 large oranges, cut in sections and lay in a dish with thinly sliced green peppers. Make a French dressing (1 tablespoon herb vinegar to 3 tablespoons oil) and stir in 1 tablespoon of finely chopped balm. Pour over the oranges and allow to marinade for a few hours before serving.

Basil

Once having used basil in cooking you will think of the two as synonymous, although the story of "Isabella and the Pot of Basil", immortalized in John Keats's poem is probably more often associated with its name. Do not let that rather grisly tale turn you aside from this truly wonderful herb, for the whole plant has a unique mouth-watering aroma which is released at the merest touch and makes you want to pick it at once and use it in all sorts of ways. The fact that it comes from India may explain the association its spicy scent has with curry.

The two varieties that are the most useful and easy to grow are sweet basil (*Ocimum basilicum*) and bush basil (*O. minimum*). They are both annuals, bush basil growing only to a height of twenty-five centimetres (ten inches) or so. If sown in a warm, sunny position in light, rich soil after the frosts, sweet basil will grow to a height of half a metre (two feet) or more until frosty weather again.

Once the plant is established, keep nipping off the tops, a process that will make it branch out and spread into a sturdy bush. The nipped tops should not be thrown away but used. Once you have let the plant flower, which it tries to do very early and is one of the reasons for nipping, it can be cut right down, and the branches hung up to dry for winter use.

Although this herb is more pungent when fresh, it retains its flavour well when dried and is always useful when cooking tomatoes. When thoroughly dry, rub the leaves and flowers off the stalks onto paper and pour into clean, dry airtight jars.

Basil is known best for its affiliation with tomatoes. It is delicious when chopped and sprinkled on circles of ice-cold, red tomatoes, on baked tomatoes, in tomato puree and in tomato juice. There are endless ways of using it with tomatoes. It is not, however, limited for using with this vegetable. It combines well with eggs, in potato salad, mixes well in a cold rice salad, and it imparts its flavour when added to soups and stews.

Cold rice salad, laced generously with chopped green herbs with basil predominating, is excellent. Boil the rice in the usual way and empty it into a colander, run cold water over it to separate the grains, leave it to drain and cool, then turn it into a bowl. There are endless varieties of ingredients to put with it from prawns, olives, nuts, grated onion and diced celery to chopped ham or bacon, asparagus tips, tomatoes and cucumber cut into chunks and slivers of cheese. Pick sprays of fresh basil from the garden, remove the leaves and chop them very finely and put them into the bowl before adding the dressing—make a French dressing in the usual way by mixing together in a cup 1 tablespoon of white vinegar or herb vinegar, and 3 tablespoons of olive or vegetable oil, salt, pepper and a dash of sugar—just before serving pour this dressing onto the rice salad and toss well.

Basil makes a savoury vinegar by packing the fresh leaves into a jar and pouring 600 ml (1 pint) of white vinegar over them. Cover tightly and allow to infuse on a sunny shelf for two weeks. Strain and use in French dressing.

French · Dressing

1 tablespoon white or herb vinegar
3 tablespoons olive oil, or your favourite oil
Salt, pepper and a pinch of sugar

Mix these ingredients together in a small basin or cup, and toss a salad with it immediately before serving.

Baked · Tomatoes · and · Basil

500 g (1 lb) tomatoes
2 onions
1 tablespoon chopped basil

Breadcrumbs
Butter, sugar, salt and pepper

Slice the tomatoes and onions. Put a layer of tomatoes in the bottom of a buttered pie dish, then a dessertspoon of basil and a layer of onions. Season with salt and pepper, a sprinkling of sugar and dot lightly with butter. Repeat this until the dish is full then top quite thickly with bread-crumbs and pieces of butter. Bake in a moderate oven for 20 minutes. The tempting aroma that greets you when this is taken from the oven is delicious. Serve it hot with roast beef or lamb.

Lamb's · Fry · with · Basil

As basil and lamb's fry go well together, the following recipe is a particularly good one.

1 lamb's fry
Flour seasoned with salt and
  pepper

2 tablespoons chopped basil
250 g (½ lb) bacon
Butter or margarine

Fry the bacon and put on a dish in a warm place. Melt the shortening, and gently cook the fry which has been cut up and rolled in the flour. At the last add the basil and 1 cup of stock and a little wine if liked. Arrange the fry with the bacon, and pour the gravy from the pan over. Serve hot.

Bay Leaves

Leaves from the Bay Tree (*Laurus nobilis*) are almost an everyday ingredient in cooking, but there is hardly any mention of the tree in gardening books or catalogues. They are not easy to obtain, and yet quite apart from their aromatic and useful leaves, the bay grows into a most attractive tree. The shape is regular and compact, and the leaves have a pleasing appearance standing neatly erect and green upon the branches. These were the leaves that were fashioned into the victor's laurel wreath of the ancients.

Doctor William Turner, a sixteenth century physician, observes that "when they are casten into the fyre they crake wonderfully". And Nicholas Culpeper in the seventeenth century wrote that "neither witch nor devil, thunder nor lightning, will hurt a man where a bay tree is".

Look after your bay tree; it is a cheerful sight when healthy, but depressing when neglected. When grown in a tub it is most ornamental. Do not let it dry out, and top-dress occasionally with well-decayed manure.

Either pick the leaves straight from the tree and use them fresh, or, if preferred, they may be dried. This is simply done by leaving them in a cool, airy place for a few days and then putting them in an airtight jar.

A bay leaf is used in a bouquet of herbs, which comprises a sprig each of thyme and parsley, and a bay leaf. These may be tied together in a muslin bag and removed before serving the dish in which they have been cooking.

You may put a bay leaf in a casserole or stew, or when boiling pickled pork or corned beef. Bay leaves are used, also, in the making of pot-pourri.

Steak · Casserole · with · Bay Leaves · and · Pickled · Walnuts

500 g (1 lb) steak	1 glass red wine or stock
4 pickled walnuts	1 finely sliced onion
2 bay leaves	1 finely sliced tomato
2 tablespoons flour	Salt, pepper and sugar

Cut steak into pieces and roll well in the flour. Put in layers in a casserole dish the steak, bay leaves, onion, tomatoes, pickled walnuts, salt, pepper and sugar to taste. (Most cooks know that sugar used sparingly helps to bring out the flavour in food.) Lastly, sprinkle any left-over flour into the casserole and pour over the wine or stock. Cover and cook in a medium oven for 2 hours.

Stuffed · Cabbage · Leaves

The following recipe for stuffed cabbage leaves is sufficient for four people, allowing two rolls for each person. The bay leaves wonderfully impart their individual aromatic flavour to the cabbage.

1 cabbage	1 breakfast cup stock
500 g (1 lb) minced steak	2 or 3 bay leaves
1 chopped onion	1 small teaspoon crushed
3/4 cup cooked rice	coriander seeds

Cut leaves carefully from the cabbage and select the most suitable for rolling the meat mixture in. Trim, put in boiling water and cook for 7 minutes. Drain in a colander.

Fry the onion in a little shortening until soft, and put in a bowl with the minced steak and rice. Season with salt and pepper, add the coriander seeds and mix well. Put a good tablespoon of this mixture onto each cabbage leaf, roll up neatly and place the rolls in a casserole dish with the bay leaves. Pour in the stock, cover and simmer gently in the oven for 45 minutes. Lift out the stuffed cabbage leaves carefully, arrange on a dish, and keep hot while the stock is thickened on the stove with a little blended cornflour.

Pour the liquid over the cabbage rolls and sprinkle them with finely chopped parsley. Serve with thick slices of crusty French bread.

Bergamot

Bergamot (*Monarda didyma*) is a perennial and is one of the most scented of all herbs. The leaves and the flowers have a delicious fragrance which bees love, and it is sometimes known as bee balm.

This herb originated in North America, and received its botanical name from Nicolas Monardes, a Spanish physician who discovered it in the sixteenth century.

There are several varieties of *Monarda*, all popular in herbaceous borders, and bearing pale blue, pink, mauve or scarlet flowers. It is the latter, Cambridge Scarlet, which is the most popular. It grows to one and a quarter metres (four feet) in the right position, and being similar to the mint family it is happiest in a shady, rather moist position.

After flowering it dies right down and should be cut to the ground, when new leaves soon appear. The clump must be watered well in dry weather or it will die right out.

With the coming of spring and warmer weather the flower stalks rapidly begin to grow taller every day. At this time a dressing of well-decayed poultry manure helps growth, and in early summer the wonderful heads of scarlet pom-poms begin to bloom. These are full of honey, and are edible. A tossed green salad with shredded bergamot flowers added at the last not only delights the eye, but tastes excellent too. The flavour is not cloying or sweet, but delicately pungent.

The young leaves are also added to salad, and they impart an elusive flavour to cooking. They combine particularly well with pork, having something of the pungency of sage, and yet the scent of rosemary as well.

It is interesting to know that oil of bergamot does not come from this plant, but from a citrus tree, the bergamot orange (*Citrus bergamia*). The flavour is similar, which is the reason for this herb's everyday name.

Pork · Sausages · with · Apple and · Bergamot

750 g (1½ lb) good pork sausages	*1 sliced onion*
	2 cloves garlic
2 large, sliced cooking apples	*1 tablespoon chopped bergamot*
30 g (1 oz) butter or margarine	*leaves*
	Flour, cinnamon, salt and
1 cup water or stock	*pepper*

Fry the apple (the peel may be left on for added flavour), onion and garlic in the shortening until soft, and remove from the pan. Roll the sausages in flour and fry until brown.

Place in alternate layers in a casserole dish the apple, onion and garlic mixture, the sausages, bergamot leaves, salt, pepper and a light dusting of cinnamon. Pour over the stock or water, cover and simmer for 1½ hours.

Bergamot · Salad · as · an
Accompaniment · to · Brawn

1 large or medium lettuce	3 bergamot flower heads
1 dessertspoon young bergamot	4 hard-boiled eggs
leaves	French dressing

Wash the lettuce and dry it thoroughly. A good idea is to do this some hours before needing it, and then put it in a covered dish in the refrigerator, it is then cool and crisp when wanted.

Wash the young bergamot leaves which may be left whole, but if possible do not wash the flowers as some of the scent is then lost.

Rub a wooden bowl with a clove of garlic, put in the torn lettuce leaves, bergamot leaves and sliced hard-boiled eggs. Add the French dressing (1 tablespoon herb vinegar to 3 tablespoons olive or your favourite oil, salt, pepper and a little sugar) and toss well. At the last tear the heads of the bergamot flowers into the salad, toss again and serve.

Oswego · Tea

A famous refreshing tea was made from the bergamot leaves in Oswego, America, known as Oswego tea. During hot weather a few leaves, either fresh or dried, may be added when infusing ordinary package tea, and will be found refreshing and beneficial.

Bergamot · Sauce

1 tablespoon chopped shallots	1 dessertspoon flour
30 g (1 oz) butter or margarine	1 dessertspoon chopped bergamot
1 wineglass white wine	leaves
Juice of ½ lemon	Salt and pepper

Melt the shortening and fry the shallots until soft, add the flour and stir until blended, then slowly add the wine and lemon juice. When thickened stir in the bergamot leaves, salt and pepper, and cook for a little longer. Serve hot. This is delicious with roast pork.

Borage

Borage (*Borago officinalis*) was esteemed more highly once than it is now. It was firmly believed that a conserve of the flowers drove away melancholy and made people merry and glad. Although it is possibly a flight of fancy to think so, perhaps there is an unknown alchemy in the plant that does do this, as all parts of this herb were known to be beneficial. The leaves, besides being a pot herb and used in salads, were also an ingredient in a "cosmetic bath", which was not only a bath to cleanse, but to strengthen the body and beautify the skin.

Borage is also one of the bee plants, and the young leaves are excellent in fruit drinks and claret cup, having a distinct cucumber flavour.

Once the seed is sown in the spring and the plant is established, there will always be borage in the garden, and although an annual, it often flowers right through the winter. It is a charming, little plant growing so demurely the blue head slightly bowed like that of some medieval lady.

The flowers are five-pointed Madonna-blue stars, the colour often used by old masters to paint the robes of Christ's mother. This is the flower featured in old needle-work, and it would be delightful to see it come back into favour. Humble though it is, it has the everlasting appeal of all humble things. There is also a rare white-flowering variety.

The method for crystallizing borage flowers, as described in the following paragraph, is the same as for violets, mint leaves, carnation petals and tiny whole rosebuds. Rose petals may be preserved in this way too, or in the alternative way described in the section on Roses. It is simple and interesting to do. It is always a joy when the flowers are ready to pack into their separate jars and are put on a shelf to catch a stray glint of sunlight. They are much too pretty to shut away in a dark cupboard. The combination of glass, sunlight and glistening flower preserved in its true colour has a fascination that no bought confectionery ever has. It is wise to keep an eye open for the right kind of jar. A suggestion is to start a collection of old apothecary jars, or the glass-stoppered ones on a fairly long stem still sometimes found in sweet shops. A helpful hint is to buy a cooking thermometer for gauging the heat of the candying liquid.

Crystallized · Flowers

The quantity of sugar and water needed for crystallizing 2 heaped tablespoons of borage flowers or 1 bunch of large violets, is 500 g (1 lb) of castor sugar and 1 cup of water.

Put the sugar and water in a saucepan over a steady heat and bring to the boil. Have the thermometer ready standing in a jug of hot water. Lift out and stand it in the saucepan until the syrup reaches 115°C (240°F). Put the thermometer back into the hot water and drop the dry flowers into the syrup, about 1 dozen at a time. Boil at 115°C (240°F) or a little more for 1 minute. Lift out the flowers with a perforated spoon and lay them carefully on a sheet of aluminium foil. Place in a slightly warmed oven and leave to cool, turning once during the process.

Instead of throwing the left-over syrup away it is a good idea to use it in a caramel custard.

Caramel · Custard

Boil the syrup further until it turns to caramel, then pour into a fireproof dish turning it quickly to cover the bottom and sides. Makes a custard with 2 eggs, 1 tablespoon of sugar, and 450 ml (¾ pint) of milk, and pour onto the caramel. Stand in a baking dish of water and cook in a moderate oven until set. It may be served chilled and topped with whipped cream decorated with crystallized flowers.

A · Cosmetic · Bath
(From "The Toilet of Flora" in The Scented Garden, *by E. S. Rohde.)*

Take 1 kg (2 lb) of barley or bean-meal, 4 kg (8 lb) of bran, and a few handfuls of borage leaves. Boil these ingredients in a sufficient quantity of spring water. Nothing cleanses and softens the skin like this bath.

Chervil

Chervil (*Anthriscus cerefolium*) is a small, thirty centimetre (one foot) high biennial herb with delicate fernlike leaves. Its rather nondescript appearance is misleading as it has great culinary value, and you will find that you can never grow enough of this plant. It is grown successfully in semi-shade in summer, but it does like the winter sun, a factor which presents a problem. If it is planted where annual herbs will protect it through the hot months, by the time winter comes the annuals are out of the way and it then benefits from the sunshine.

Always pick the leaves from the outside as with parsley, allowing it to keep on growing from the centre.

This herb is particularly suitable for growing in a pot or trough. A good spot is the kitchen window-sill where it is within easy reach to pick and cut up for salads, mashed potato, and especially scrambled egg, when its nearness is appreciated for early breakfasts.

The leaves have a fresh yet spicy taste, and although it certainly does not take the place of parsley, it may, with great advantage, be used instead,

adding a different flavour to familiar food. It is excellent with omelettes and in soups. Other suggestions are:

A tossed French salad with as much chopped chervil as you can spare sprinkled on the top before serving.

Diced cold potato mixed together with a light mayonnaise dressing and a generous amount of chervil.

Iced tomato soup garnished with thin slices of lemon and finely chopped chervil.

Haricot beans served piping hot with a piquant sauce, and chervil added at the last.

Nicholas Culpeper aptly describes chervil in his *Complete Herbal* written in the seventeenth century:

"The garden chervil doth at first somewhat resemble parsley, but after it is better grown the leaves are cut in and jagged, resembling hemlock, being a little hairy, and of a whitish green colour, sometimes turning reddish in the summer, with the stalks also; it riseth a little above half a foot high, bearing white flowers in spiked tufts, which turn into long and round seeds pointed at the ends, and blackish when they are ripe . . ."

Haricot · Beans · with · Tomatoes

This is excellent in the winter when fresh vegetables are often scarce and is quite sufficient on its own with the main meat course.

500 g (1 lb) haricot beans	*2 crushed cloves garlic*
500 g (1 lb) tomatoes	*1 dessertspoon brown sugar*
4 shallots	*2 tablespoons chervil*
125 g (4 oz) butter or	*Salt and pepper*
margarine	

Pour boiling water over the beans and soak overnight. Simmer in salted water until soft (about 1½ hours). Drain.

Wash the shallots and cut them up finely leaving as much of the green part as possible for colour and flavour. Put them with the garlic into a frying pan with the melted shortening. Simmer gently until soft. Peel and chop up the tomatoes and with the sugar, salt and pepper add to the frying pan. Cook a little longer, then pour the puree onto the beans and heat through. Just before serving stir in the chervil.

To vary, emulate the famous dish cassoulet, which originates from the rich farming country of south-west France, by adding to the beans 250 g (½ lb) fried, lean bacon cut into pieces, or 500 g (1 lb) of sliced garlic sausage, pour the mixture into a casserole, top with buttered breadcrumbs and brown slowly in the oven.

Potato · Soup

500 g (1 lb) potatoes	*1 dessertspoon flour blended*
1 onion	*with milk*
Chervil	*Little cream*
1 pint stock or water	*Salt and pepper*

Wash and slice the potato and onion, and simmer on the stove in the liquid until the vegetables are soft.

Rub through a sieve and return to the stove with the blended flour. Bring to the boil, and pour into hot soup plates. Add thin cream, fried *croûtons* and 1 teaspoon chopped chervil to each serving.

Chicory

Chicory (*Cichorium intybus*), also known as witloof, or succory as it was once called, is regarded more as a vegetable or pot herb, although it is delicious when a tablespoon of the finely shredded leaves are added to a lettuce salad. The leaves have a slightly bitter yet pleasant taste, and are esteemed for their health-giving properties.

Culpeper says of it: "A handful of the leaves or roots, boiled in wine or water, and drank fasting, drives forth choleric and phlegmatic humours."

The plant can grow to over two metres (six feet) high, and in the autumn the china-blue flowers are carried on long spires, making a welcome show of colour in the herb garden at this time of year.

As well as having medicinal uses, the roots are dried and ground to mix with coffee, and may be boiled like parsnips and eaten as a vegetable.

Plant seeds in the spring; give this large plant plenty of room to grow.

Chicory · and · Eggs

This is an up-to-date version of an old recipe of three hundred years ago. Serves two.

Blanch 2 heads of chicory leaves for 6 minutes in boiling water. Drain and squeeze out the moisture. Cut them with a knife and put in a saucepan with a little stock and a bunch of chopped savoury herbs (marjoram, parsley and thyme for instance) and simmer for ¼ hour. Thicken with a little blended cornflour and turn onto a serving dish. Keep hot while poaching 4 eggs to lay upon the cooked chicory. Serve at once.

Chicory · Salad

1 lettuce
1 chicory leaf
1 doz. stoned black olives
8 anchovies
4 hard-boiled eggs
1 cup diced celery

4 peeled tomatoes cut into
  quarters
1 tablespoon chopped chervil
  and chives in equal parts
French dressing

Chop the fresh, chicory leaf and put with the torn-up lettuce in a bowl that has been rubbed with a cut clove of garlic. Add all ingredients except the herbs, anchovies and hard-boiled eggs and toss well. Arrange the halved eggs with an anchovy on each one on top of the salad, and sprinkle with herbs. Serve with cold meat and French bread for lunch, or alfresco on a hot summer night.

Chives

Chives (*Allium schoenoprasum*) belongs to the same family as the onion, leek, garlic and shallot. The thin, grass-like leaves have a delicate taste of onion, and are generally used to flavour cream cheese, salads and omelettes.

Chives makes an attractive border, the flowers are decorative, looking like little mauve pincushions, and are charming in a mixed posy.

If both the leaves and the flowers are picked continually, the plant is improved by growing more vigorously and having a better flavour. Chives may suddenly die out and disappear, so divide the bulbs in the autumn to

prevent overcrowding, water them in dry weather and top-dress twice a year with old poultry humus.

If raising the plant from seed, sow in the spring. It grows successfully on a kitchen window-sill, and has the added advantage of being within easy reach when needed.

Chives and cream cheese have an affinity. Chop the chives finely and mash them into the cream cheese with salt, pepper, a little cream and a squeeze of lemon juice. Spread on savouries and in sandwiches or pat into a mound in the centre of a serving dish and surround with biscuits; supply a knife and let everyone help themselves to this savoury mixture either as a before-dinner appetizer, or to eat afterwards.

Another suggestion is to add a tablespoon of chopped chives to mashed potato, particularly when accompanying grilled chops, steak, or crumbed cutlets. In scrambled eggs, or in an omelette, chives are equally delicious. The uses of this herb are many and varied, especially to the imaginative cook.

Cucumber and chives combine well, and the first recipe to follow— Creamed Cucumber—is excellent.

Creamed · Cucumber

2 green cucumbers, or	*1 cup white sauce*
6 apple cucumbers	*Salt and pepper*
1 tablespoon chopped chives	

Peel the cucumbers, cut into cubes, put into boiling water and cook a few minutes. Drain. Make a white sauce with 1½ tablespoons of butter, 2 level tablespoons of flour and 1 cup of milk. Stir in the cucumber, chives, salt and pepper. Heat through and serve hot.

French · Omelette · with · Chives

Those who own a correct omelette pan, heavy with a flat bottom and shallow with sloping sides, are fortunate; however a successful omelette may still be made in an ordinary frying pan. Experienced cooks say that one omelette should never contain more than six egg and in some recipe books there are whole pages devoted to the art of omelette-making. I find it easier to make several, one for each person, unless making the omelette for two people, in which case six eggs may be used. This omelette recipe serves one.

3 eggs
1 oz butter
Chives, salt and pepper, extra butter

Dissolve the butter over a medium heat. Meanwhile, break the eggs into a bowl and whisk well but lightly. Season with salt and pepper, add two tiny cubes of butter and the chives.

When the butter is sizzling gently, see that it is distributed evenly over the pan, and pour in the eggs. With a knife quickly lift up the sides of the omelette all round the pan allowing the mixture to run underneath. Do this several times, and cut it once across the middle. The bottom of the omelette should be set and a golden brown, the top creamy and not quite cooked. Lift the omelette with an egg slice, fold it over and slide it onto a hot plate and serve immediately.

Fish · Pie · with · Herbs

3 cups cooked flaked fish	1 dessertspoon chopped walnuts
1½ cups white sauce	Salt, pepper, grated nutmeg
1 tablespoon chopped chives	
1 dessertspoon chopped parsley	

Stir the fish into the white sauce. Season with salt, pepper and nutmeg. Put into a fireproof dish and top with herbs and walnuts. Brown in a medium oven and serve with slices of lemon and very thin brown bread and butter.

Coriander

Coriander (*Coriandrum sativum*) is an annual and is grown for its aromatic seeds which must be allowed to ripen before using, as they are unpleasant when fresh. The aromatic foliage and roots are also useful, especially in Asian and Middle Eastern cooking.

Sow the seed in the spring, when the plant will soon grow to about sixty centimetres (two feet). After flowering, collect the seeds and allow to dry, or leave to ripen on the plant, but do not wait too long otherwise they will all drop off.

Coriander is one of our more musical words, bringing to the imagination medieval gardens where the names of flowers were strung together like garlands; coriander, cumin and southernwood; rue, elecampane and tansy; costmary, cowslips and gilliflowers. It also conjures up the richness of the East and the pageantry of the Old Testament, of gold, frankincense and myrrh. It is as old as the Bible, and is mentioned in Exodus, ch. 16, v. 31:

"And the house of Israel called the name thereof Manna: and it was like coriander seed, white; and the taste of it was like wafers made with honey."

The fragrant seeds are an ingredient in both curry powder and pot-pourri, and are often added to give a spicy flavour to food. A teaspoon of crushed seeds gives a subtle undertone to casseroles and soups.

Spiced · Tea · Cake

1 tablespoon butter	*1 peeled thinly sliced apple*
½ cup sugar	*1 dessertspoon pounded*
1 egg	*coriander seed*
1 cup milk	*A little sugar and nutmeg*
1 cup self-raising flour	

Cream the butter and sugar. Add the egg and beat well. Gently fold in the sifted flour and milk alternately.

Smear a cake tin with butter and then a dusting of flour. (This prevents the cake from sticking.) Lay the sliced apple in the bottom of the tin, and sprinkle with sugar, nutmeg and pounded coriander seed. Pour the batter over and bake in a moderate oven until cooked, about ½ hour. Carefully loosen the cake from the sides of the tin, and turn onto a plate or wire-cooler. It is delicious when hot, but may be eaten cold with thick cream.

Baked · Veal · Chops

Pound 2 cloves of garlic and 2 teaspoons coriander seed together, and mix with breadcrumbs. Dip chops in flour, egg and seasoned breadcrumbs, put in baking dish with a little oil and the grated rind of ½ lemon. Cook in a moderate oven until brown and crisp.

Crumbed bananas may, with advantage, be added to the baking dish 15 minutes before serving.

Marmalade · Flavoured · with Coriander

4 oranges	2 kg (4 lb) sugar
2 lemons	1 tablespoon crushed coriander
6 cups water	seed

Cut up the oranges and lemons and soak in water for 12 hours. Bring to the boil and put in the coriander seed tied in a muslin bag. When the peel is tender slowly add the warmed sugar, and boil until the mixture jellies. Remove the muslin bag before putting the marmalade in jars.

The coriander seed will impart a spicy fragrance to the usually prosaic marmalade.

Dill

Dill (*Anethum graveolens*) is a tall annual growing to a height of one metre (three feet) and over. Its lacy leaves are delicately aromatic, and when chopped up finely they give potato salads and cucumber sandwiches an interesting new flavour.

Sow the seed in the spring after frosts, where the plants are to remain, and thin out later, leaving thirty centimetres (a foot) between each. It is unwise to plant dill near fennel, for when you come to collect the seeds you will find that the mature plants are so similar in appearance and flavour that it will take time and close examination to sort them out satisfactorily. Dill is a more delicate plant in every way; the stalk is finer and the leaves have a more subtle flavour, reminiscent of carraway. Fennel is more like aniseed, and the seed-heads are smaller and not as heavy and full as dill.

Dill water is well known for soothing babies, and as early as Saxon times it was used for this purpose.

Dill pickles are a delicious and popular continental food. Dill sauce with fish is excellent, and it is also one of the herbs that may be used with advantage in scrambled eggs and mashed potatoes. The pale-yellow flower-heads, too, are pretty enough to bring inside and arrange in a mixed bowl, having an airy appearance and the simple charm of wayside flowers.

Scallops · with · Dill

Roll 500 g (1 lb) of scallops in flour, egg and breadcrumbs, and fry in 125 g (¼ lb) of melted butter or margarine for a few minutes on either side. Put scallops in a dish and keep hot. Stir 1 good tablespoon of flour into the shortening, adding a little more if necessary, and blend well over medium heat. Pour 1 scant cup of stock or milk and 1 tablespoon sherry into the pan and stir until thick. Add 1 tablespoon of finely chopped dill, and pour the sauce over the scallops. Serve at once.

Coleslaw · with · Dill

Coleslaw or cabbage salad is economical to make and tasty to eat in the summer either by itself with cold meat or served with other salads; it also goes equally as well with hot food in the winter.

1 small firm cabbage	1 breakfast cup of mayonnaise
2 tablespoons chopped dill	(the readymade kind sold in
1 chopped green apple	shops is quick and easy)

Trim and wash the cabbage, cut it into four and shred it as thinly as possible; the finer it is cut the better it is. Put the shredded cabbage into boiling salted water and boil for 5 minutes, then tip it into a colander and run cold water over it for a few minutes. Let the cabbage drain thoroughly, shaking it occasionally. When it is quite free of water put it into a bowl with the dill and apple, pour the dressing over and mix the salad well. It may be left overnight in the refrigerator with a plate over the top to prevent any odour from the cabbage affecting other food.

Fennel

Sweet fennel (*Foeniculum vulgare*) is a perennial, while Florence or finochio fennel (*F. vulgare dulce*) is an annual. The latter is more popular; not only are both the leaves and seeds used, but the base of the stems, which are bulbous, are either eaten raw like celery, or are gently boiled until tender and served with white sauce.

Grow Florence fennel in a sunny position and give it plenty of moisture. When the base begins to swell, cultivate and feed the soil.

In appearance fennel resembles dill, although usually not growing so high. The leaves and seeds are similar in flavour, fennel being more pungent, and distinctly reminiscent of aniseed.

There are many legends and beliefs surrounding this herb, and it has been mentioned by poets and writers throughout the centuries. One of its virtues was supposed to be that of restoring eyesight, another, to reduce overweight.

The chopped leaves of fennel are used in a sauce for fish, or a sprig may be placed inside the fish when grilling or baking.

The bulbous stalk is eaten in various ways, perhaps the most tasty being a salad made of the sliced, nutty, raw fennel tossed together with French dressing and a dessertspoon of finely chopped chervil. This is something different and delicious in the way of salads, and is excellent with cold chicken.

The continental vegetable markets are famous for their colourful and tempting varieties of vegetables—heaped white bunches of Florence fennel, eggplant or aubergines, green and red peppers, broccoli, globe artichokes, endives, small marrows or courgettes, and so on. Warm climates are ideal for all these Mediterranean vegetables, which are now readily available.

Cooked · Fennel

Pull the fennel from the ground and cut away the leafy tops (put them in the refrigerator wrapped in foil for using some other time), wash well and cut into pieces. Simmer gently until tender. Drain. Make a white sauce and add the cooked fennel. Heat through and stir in a dessertspoon of chopped parsley before serving.

Fennel · Cream · Sauce
(For fish)

1 cup cream	2 tablespoons finely chopped
1 tablespoon lemon juice	fennel leaves
1 teaspoon honey	Salt and pepper

Whip cream until thickened but not too fluffy, stir in the honey and lemon, blending well. Add fennel and seasoning last.

Fennel-Seed · Sausage

A homemade sausage eaten cold is delicious and also nourishing, as well as being economical. With a good basic recipe, there can always be variations in the flavour and meat. For instance, 1 kg (2 lb) of sausage meat could be substituted for 1 kg (2 lb) of minced steak. Less fennel seeds may be used. Garlic, onion, and parsley may all be added separately, or together. It is entirely a matter of taste. This recipe is simple, and is such a family favourite that it vanishes almost immediately.

1 kg (2 lb) minced steak	*2 level tablespoons of fennel*
2 eggs	*seeds*
4 cups soft breadcrumbs	*1 chopped onion, salt and*
	pepper

Put the meat, breadcrumbs, fennel seeds and onion in a bowl, add the beaten eggs and mix well together. Have ready a clean floured cloth. Form the mixture into a sausage on the cloth, and roll the cloth well round, tying each end with string. Put into a large saucepan of boiling water, and boil for 2½ hours. Lift out carefully, onto a plate, unfold the cloth and slip it away from the sausage, roll in dry breadcrumbs and leave to cool.

Garlic

Garlic (*Allium sativum*) should definitely have a place in the store cupboard, for the discreet use of this pungent herb improves many dishes. The bulb is the part that is used. This is made up of separate sections called cloves, and covered by a light skin, which is peeled before using.

Garlic was once known as a valuable medicinal herb, and today it is still highly regarded by many people for having a beneficial effect on the digestive system and for improving the complexion. There is a herb farm in England that sells garlic specially prepared in capsule form for this purpose.

If you like garlic, it is a temptation to use it quite lavishly, and to eat it raw, perhaps finely sliced on bread with cheese. This is a dangerous practice for the effects stay for a long time and is rather hard on other people! Unless contemplating a day or two of solitude, it might be wise to follow Bottom's counsel in *A Midsummer Night's Dream*, "eat no onions nor garlic, for we are to utter sweet breath". A clove of garlic rubbed round a wooden salad bowl, or garlic butter spread on a hot French loaf is usually sufficient when using it raw.

When cooked, especially for a long time, garlic imparts its fragrance to the dish, while not being in any way offensive to those who are prejudiced against it. It is astonishing how many cloves may be used in one dish, with the addition of shallots, without making it overwhelming, providing it is cooked long and slowly.

Garlic belongs to the the same family as the shallot, onion, chives, leek and rocambole. Grow it in rich, friable soil, planting the cloves to a depth of 5 centimetres (2 inches) and 15 centimetres (6 inches) apart, in early spring. Keep the bed weeded and watered. The bulbs may be lifted and stored the following late summer or early autumn, the best of the cloves being kept on one side for planting again at the right time.

There are numerous ways of using garlic. Here are three suggestions that will be found particularly helpful.

1. When roasting lamb or mutton, especially if it seems to be a little tough, make one or two incisions in the raw meat with a knife and insert small cloves of garlic. It seems to act as a tenderizer as well as deliciously flavouring the meat.

2. Rub a small square of bread on both sides with garlic and place at the bottom of the salad bowl with the lettuce on top. By the time you come to toss it, the aroma will have penetrated the lettuce.

3. Chop 6 cloves of garlic very finely until it is almost pulp, then mash it into 250g (½ lb) softened butter. Spread on slices of hot crusty French bread and serve in a basket with any luncheon dish.

Casserole · Sausages · in · Cider

8 sausages	1 cup of cider
2 apples	Herbs, salt and pepper
4 shallots	2 tablespoons of flour
2 or 3 cloves of garlic	

Roll the sausages well in flour and fry them lightly all over in a little cooking oil. Put them in a casserole dish with layers of sliced apple, cored but not peeled, finely chopped shallots (do not discard the green part, it is edible and adds colour), finely chopped garlic and some sage and parsley. Season with salt and pepper. Add a cup of cider. Cover and cook in a medium oven for 1 hour.

I find butcher's sausages best to use, they are more meaty as a rule, making this a nourishing and savoury meal.

Stuffed · Steak · Rolls
750 g (1½ lb) round steak
1 cup of stock, water or red wine

Stuffing

1 cup of soft breadcrumbs
2 rashers of bacon cut into small pieces
2 cloves of finely chopped garlic
1 dessertspoon each of chopped onion, celery and parsley
1 tablespoon of melted butter

Cut the steak into strips. Combine the stuffing and spread on the strips. Roll up and secure with wooden toothpicks. Roll lightly in flour and brown in a little shortening. Add the liquid, and simmer in a medium oven for 2 hours.

Lavender

Nearly every garden has at least one lavender bush. It is not surprising that this beautifully scented small shrub has kept its popularity throughout the centuries, from long before the Christian era up to the present time.

There is no scent quite like lavender, each spray containing the warm, sweet smell of summer. Shakespeare, in *The Winter's Tale*, calls it "hot lavender":

> *Here's flowers for you;*
> *Hot lavender, mints, savory, marjoram;*
> *The marigold, that goes to bed wi' the sun,*
> *And with him rises weeping...*

Even on the bleakest winter's day, when a dried lavender flower or a lavender sachet is held and inhaled for a moment, a picture immediately forms of long, drowsy days, humming bees and a glowing tapestry of flowers in the garden.

Lavender is a *xerophyte*, which means that it is especially adapted for living in dry conditions. The grey leaves indicate this quality, the greyness really being a mass of tiny white hairs, which are there to hold moisture within the plant. This is a planting guide to many grey leaved plants, sage being another, also the old-fashioned herbaceous border favourite lychnis, although if you were to snap any of these leaves in half you would find that they are green inside. Do not feel that rich soil will prevent a lavender bush from growing well. As long as it is well-drained and not in clay soil, it will flourish. Working a little lime around the roots will benefit the plant under these conditions.

Pot-pourri is not complete without lavender, which retains its perfume long after the other flowers have faded, with the exception of rosemary. These two plants have strong, natural aromatic oils, which are known and valued by chemical firms and are extracted for use in commerce.

The two common varieties are *Lavandula dentata*, and *L. vera*. The first is generally known as French lavender, and grows into a large bushy shrub with grey, serrated leaves and pale mauve blossoms. It likes a sunny position and light sandy soil, and is almost always in bloom, its main flush being in the winter. It is recommended to use as a hedge, and grows exceptionally well on a stone wall.

L. vera is the English lavender, and there are other varieties closely resembling it known as *L. officinalis* and *L. spica*. It is a small-growing shrub, its smooth grey leaves are narrow and pointed, and the flowers which bloom in summer grow in long spikes of deep mauve. The scent of English lavender is incomparable, and for a low hedge it is ideal.

L. stoechas is also known as French lavender, and was once called by the quaint old name of sticadove. This dwarf variety is not often seen. It blooms in the spring and is worth growing for this reason and for its rich, purple flower-heads, similar in form to *L. dentata*. There is also a white flowering lavender, *L. officinalis alba*, which is rare and very sweet.

Any leaf or flower that comes from a lavender bush should never be wasted. When blooms that have been picked, are spent, they may be tied in bunches to perfume drawers and linen cupboards, or added to the pot-pourri bowl, together with the aromatic leaves. Lavender should be pruned after flowering, to ensure a healthy well-shaped shrub. The prunings, of course, should not be wasted either. When lavender cuttings are put in sand, two-thirds of each cutting should be stripped of its leaves; these leaves are gathered up and put straight into the large earthenware jar that always contains pot-pourri.

Long ago lavender was used not only for making scented articles, but in confectionery, cooking and in medicine. There are delightful old recipes for lavender wine, lavender sugar, lavender water, lavender tea, the distilling of lavender for the volatile oil, as well as directions for making lavender fans, lavender bags and lavender quilted into caps. One charming idea that could be used today is to spear sweets and small pieces of fruit with spikes of English lavender.

An · Aromatic · Bath

This is a simplified version of an old recipe:

Boil for 5 minutes, in a sufficient quantity of water, one or all of the following plants: bay leaves, thyme, rosemary, marjoram, lavender, wormwood, pennyroyal, balm and eau-de-Cologne mint. Strain and add a little brandy. Shake the required quantity into a hot bath.

Lavender · Sugar

In the seventeenth century a favourite confectionery was Lavender Sugar, made by beating lavender flowers into three times their weight in sugar. If you put two or three lavender heads into the sugar canister it will scent the sugar beautifully.

Lavender · Water · without Distillation
(From "The Toilet of Flora" in The Scented Garden, by E. S. Rohde.)

If you would have speedily, without the trouble of distillation, a water impregnated with the flavour of Lavender, put two or three drops of Oil of Spike, and a lump of Sugar, into a pint of clear Water, or Spirit of Wine, and shake them well together in a glass phial, with a narrow neck. This Water, though not distilled, is very fragrant.

Lavender · Vinegar

If you desire lavender vinegar to give a subtle fragrance to salads, steep lavender heads in 600 ml (1 pint) of white vinegar in a glass container on a sunny shelf for 2 weeks. Strain and use.

Although the little-known plant often called lavender cotton or French lavender (*Santolina chamae cyparissus*) does not belong to the lavender family at all, it may be included here to bring up the rear of the lavenders. With its fragrant foliage, resembling delicate grey coral, and round yellow flowers, it is a decorative and charming addition to any garden. It likes to grow in the same type of soil as the lavenders, light and well drained in a sunny position where it will attain a height of one metre (three feet) with a spreading habit. Do not prune heavily.

Sprays of this herb were once laid in drawers to keep away moths, and oil for perfume from the plant is used industrially. The leaves and flowers are valuable in potpourri, adding colour as well as scent.

Marjoram

There are many different species of the valuable culinary herb marjoram, the most popular variety being the sweet marjoram (*Origanum majorana*).

Marjoram is a perennial and very easy to grow. Sow the seed in spring, or propagate by root division. It likes a sunny, well-drained position, and if cut back after flowering, will grow into a healthy, shrubby plant about sixty centimetres (two feet) high. When winter frosts have driven basil from the herb garden, marjoram comes into its own. It is difficult to choose between these two herbs for savoury flavour. Marjoram is more subtle, not giving its aroma as freely as basil. A light touch of the hand, or spray from the hose will release the fragrance of basil, but you must pick a stalk of marjoram, when the soft and scented leaves will tempt you to nibble and enjoy their pungency.

Marjoram may be used in a number of ways and it is wise to have more than one bush growing. Delicious brown-bread sandwiches are made with marjoram leaves spread thickly on a bed of cream cheese. Use the leaves in herb scones (a family favourite), in salads, omelettes and sauces, in vinegars, sweet bags and pot-pourri. There is also the customary bouquet of herbs for flavouring soups and stews, in which thyme, parsley, marjoram and a bay leaf are usually recommended.

Although marjoram was once used medicinally for a number of complaints—from digestive disorders to curing toothache—it was also highly valued as a "strewing" herb on the floors of houses.

Marjoram is more pungent, perhaps, when dried than it is fresh. Although fresh herbs are probably superior, it is sometimes more convenient to use dried herbs, even when the former is available. When marjoram is just beginning to flower, cut some of it for drying, and proceed as described earlier for drying herbs.

Cottage · Pie

This familiar dish is sometimes called Shepherd's Pie, another homely old name, indicating the popularity of the dish over the years. It consists of minced meat with a topping of mashed potato, and is always appetizing whether perfectly plain with only the addition of gravy and a little onion to the meat, or flavoured in a number of different ways. It is important to have the mashed potato crisp and golden. This recipe is for fresh meat, but it could be made with minced left-over meat and a cup of gravy, omitting the cup of liquid and the flour.

4 shallots	*1 cup stock or water*
2 rashers bacon	*1 tablespoon chopped marjoram*
1 clove garlic	*leaves*
500 g (1 lb) minced steak	*Salt and pepper*
1 tablespoon flour	*500 g (1 lb) mashed potatoes*

Wash and cut up the shallots, using as much of the green part as possible. Chop the garlic very finely. Cut the bacon into small pieces. Heat some oil in a large frying pan and cook these ingredients until soft. Add marjoram leaves and the minced steak. Press down with a fork, and brown all over, mixing the contents of the pan well together. Add the flour, cook a little longer, then pour in the liquid. Season. Turn into an oven-proof dish and top with creamy mashed potato. A tablespoon of nutty sesame seeds and pieces of butter spread over the potato before putting it in the oven is excellent. Bake in a medium oven for ¾ hour. If the top is not browned enough turn on the griller for a few minutes before serving.

Herb · Scones

While picking a bunch of parsley one day, a neighbour gave me this delicious recipe for using it in scones to put on top of a bubbling casserole or stew, half an hour before serving. In fact any savoury herb may be used that seems best suited to the dish it is accompanying, and in winter it is particularly nourishing. When roasting pork, mix rosemary leaves (cut up finely with the kitchen scissors) into the scones and bake on a tray in the oven. Served dry like this they are appropriate with a rich meat.

1 cup self-raising flour
60 g (2 oz) butter

2 tablespoons chopped
marjoram leaves
Pinch salt and a little cold
water

Sift flour and salt. Rub in the butter. Add marjoram and enough cold water to make a stiff dough. Stir quickly and lightly with a knife and then pat out on the table with your hand. Cut into squares and use straight away, or wrap in foil and put in the refrigerator until needed.

Burning · Steak

This way of preparing fillet steak is different, and fun to do. The flavour of the burnt brandy, and the aromatic marjoram leaves sprinkled over the cooked steak, makes it a meal to be enjoyed.

4 pieces of fillet steak
½ cup brandy

2 tablespoons finely chopped
marjoram leaves
Butter, salt and pepper

Melt butter in a heavy frying pan and put in the steaks. Let them sizzle, turn them over and cook a little longer. Pour the brandy over and set alight. When the flames have died down put the steaks on a hot dish. Pour liquor from the pan over, dust with salt and freshly ground pepper, and top with the marjoram leaves.

Potato · Pie

If you decide to serve one vegetable with a meal, potatoes with marjoram is quite substantial.

500 g (1 lb) potatoes
4 shallots

2 tablespoons marjoram leaves
125 g (¼ lb) butter, salt and
pepper

Peel the potatoes and slice them thinly. Place in layers in a buttered pie dish the potatoes, marjoram leaves, pieces of butter and finely sliced shallots. Top with buttered breadcrumbs and cook slowly in a medium oven, about 1 hour.

Marjoram · Vinegar

Fill a glass jar with marjoram leaves and pour the best white vinegar over them. Cover and leave on a sunny shelf for 2 weeks. Strain and use.

Mint

There is a bed of mint to be found in nearly every garden. No wonder it has not vanished from our daily lives as so many other herbs have done; for besides being very hardy, the delicious, piercing quality of its scent has its own appeal.

Culpeper describes a formidable number of diseases in which preparations of this herb were used medicinally. It is mentioned in the New Testament and mints are described in early English plant lists.

Mint was valued for scenting baths and to "strengthen the sinews" at the same time. It was also used as a strewing herb, in teas and in confectionery. A few sprigs of mint boiled with new potatoes is believed to make them more digestible.

There are many varieties of mint, the best known being spearmint (*Mentha spicata*). It is interesting to grow other kinds as well. Applemint (*M. rotundifolia*), which smells strongly of apples, is recommended for mint sauce.

Eau-de-Cologne mint (*M. piperita citrata*), sometimes known as berga-mot mint, has dark purplish leaves with an aroma definitely reminiscent of eau-de-Cologne. Put a sprig in the saucepan when cooking peas, and enjoy the scent that fills the kitchen, and at the same time delicately permeates the peas. This particular mint makes a refreshing tea on hot days.

The lower-growing peppermint or menthol (*M. piperita officinalis*) is the true Mitcham peppermint, and the oil from this plant is used commercially. A tisane made from menthol is highly esteemed for its beneficial effects when suffering from a cold.

Pennyroyal (*M. pulegium*), once valued for ridding rooms of fleas, is a pretty little edging or rockery plant with circlets of mauve flowers on miniature spires in spring. Its leaves, smelling and tasting of peppermint, are excellent when used with new potatoes and butter.

The curly mint (*M. spicata crispata*), with its crinkly leaves, is used in mint sauce and is most attractive and tastes delicious when crystallized.

All the mints like fairly rich soil and plenty of water, and as they have rampant root systems, it is wise to give them room to grow. If space is limited, each variety may be confined in a chimney pot buried up to the rim in the ground. Propagate by root division, preferably in winter or spring.

It is in the summer that mint is really appreciated for its fresh flavour and invigorating properties. In the making of fruit drinks it is invaluable, and some dried leaves mixed with package tea are refreshing on a very hot day.

There are many well-known ways of using mint in cooking, and the following recipes contain a few additional ideas for making a wider employment of this pleasant and beneficial herb.

For a change when making mint sauce, sweeten with honey instead of sugar, and use lemon instead of vinegar, and remember there should always be lots of mint in it.

Tasty sandwiches are made with brown bread, cream cheese and finely chopped mint leaves.

Fry bananas lightly in butter with plenty of chopped-up mint to accompany crumbed cutlets.

Minted · Egg · Tart

250 g (½ lb) cream cheese
6 eggs
3 tablespoons well-chopped
    mint

1 thinly sliced cucumber with
    the peel left on
Short pastry

Line a pie dish with a thin layer of short pastry (I have given a recipe for pastry in the chapter on sage), spread with cream cheese or cottage cheese which has been mashed with some top milk or cream, and cover with the cucumber. Break the eggs onto this, season with salt and pepper and strew the top with mint, using spearmint or applemint. Bake in a moderate oven until the pastry is golden and the eggs set, about ½ hour. This is particularly delicious in hot weather eaten cold for lunch, or to take on a picnic. A glass of icy apple cider and thin slices of cold ham or veal makes an excellent accompaniment.

Mint · Julep

Wash a large bunch of mint (eau-de-Cologne mint is especially good) and put it in a basin. Bruise it and then add 1 cup of sugar, 1 tin of pineapple juice and the juice of 4 lemons. Cover and let it stand for some hours, then strain into a tall jug. Add 3 bottles of dry ginger ale, cubes of ice, thin slices of lemon and sprigs of mint. This has been a wonderful standby for luncheon on many occasions, and is preferred by many people to wine in the middle of the day.

Mint · Jelly

45 g (1½ oz) gelatine
300 ml (½ pint) hot water
375 g (12 oz) sugar
750 ml (1¼ pints) white
  vinegar

4 tablespoons chopped mint
  (spearmint, applemint or
  curly mint)

Dissolve sugar in the vinegar by bringing to the boil and boil for 4 minutes. Dissolve gelatine in the hot water and add it with the mint and a pinch of salt to the vinegar. Bring it to the boil once more and remove immediately. Add a few drops of green colouring and allow to cool, stirring occasionally. When beginning to set put into small pots. Cover and keep in the refrigerator. Excellent with lamb, mutton, veal and pork as a change from mint sauce.

Crystallized · Mint · Leaves

Select the best leaves of curly mint, applemint or eau-de-Cologne mint. See that they are perfectly dry, and with a fine paint brush coat each one on both sides with a slightly beaten egg white, then dust all over with castor sugar. Put on waxed paper in a warm oven to dry, leaving the door half open. Turn occasionally. When quite dry and glistening greenly, nibble one or two and see how delicious and pepperminty they taste. Put them away in an airtight container between layers of waxed paper and use for garnishing sweets and cakes.

Pineapple · Cocktail

1 pineapple
2 tablespoons of finely chopped mint
1 cup of sugar

Peel the pineapple. Stand it on a plate and slice downwards with a knife until the hard core is reached. Cut the pineapple pieces into cubes. Strain the juice into a saucepan with the sugar and mint and bring to the boil and simmer for a few minutes. Pour back onto the pineapple. Chill in the refrigerator and serve as an appetizer in individual dishes garnished with a fresh sprig of mint and a cherry.

The core and peel from the pineapple may be kept and simmered with sugar and water for about ¾ hour, then the liquid strained off and refrigerated for drinks.

Oregano

A herb, highly regarded in Mediterranean cooking and one that is generally popular at the present time, is oregano (*Origanum vulgare*). One of the marjorams, the leaves are far more pungent and hot than the sweet marjoram and therefore used more sparingly. In most cases the plant or seed has been brought into Australia by immigrants from their native hillsides, the species differing slightly in some provinces. In both Greek and Italian cuisine, the dried flower-tops are mainly used.

The scent varies also, according to soil and climate. It has some resemblance to marjoram, the leaves being smaller and rougher; it has a creeping root system and a rather sprawling habit. Oregano likes to grow in light, well-drained soil in a sunny position. Seed may be sown in the spring, or the roots may be divided in the autumn, winter or spring.

A plant, cherished carefully, will multiply to grand proportions. It is not wise to nibble oregano leaves indiscriminately for the powerful flavour is quite astonishing; the scent of oregano is warm, and provokes an image of the hearty food so full of flavour that it is used in, or accompanies.

Here are some suggestions for the use of the herb.

1. Oregano should be dried when in flower for the full benefit of the aroma; stalks may be picked as they flower, hung up to dry, and then used.

2. For a tasty grilled steak, rub it first with a cut clove of garlic, and then brush melted butter on to the steak with a dried branch of oregano. Some of the leaves and tiny flowers adhere to the meat. Grill, then turn the steak and repeat the process.

3. Rub dried oregano leaves, or put them freshly chopped, on top of tomatoes when baking, grilling or frying them.

4. Serve boiled spaghetti with a sauce mixed into it made from thinly sliced cloves of garlic, fried in oil until soft, peeled tomatoes, and oregano to taste. Top with grated Parmesan cheese.

Steak · Kebabs

Allowing 250 g (½ lb) meat for each person, cut fairly thick grilling steak into bite-sized cubes. Put the cubes onto skewers alternately with pieces of tomato, bacon, pineapple and pickled onions. Season with salt, pepper and dried oregano. Grill. These kebabs are ideal for a barbecue meal, and may be eaten with crisp bread rolls or a long French loaf, garlic flavoured.

Pizza · Pie

When preparing pizza pie it is worth the trouble to make the bread dough with yeast in the traditional way for a dish loses its personality if made with "short cuts". The rich smell of the yeast, the smooth, elastic softness of the dough beneath the fingers, and the watching of it rise in a warm place all give such satisfaction that if only there were more time, making one's own bread would be a pleasurable and not difficult house-wifely task. Once there was enough dough left over from the pie to make a miniature loaf for the youngest member of the family—a wonderfully risen round loaf with a beige top which looked exactly like the illustrations in children's storybooks!

Bread Dough

125 g (¼ lb) plain flour   *7 g (¼ oz) yeast*
75 ml (⅛ pint) warm milk   *¼ teaspoon salt*
  and water mixed

Filling

4 peeled and cut tomatoes   *1 dessertspoon fresh finely*
1 tin anchovy fillets   *chopped oregano*
125 g (4 oz) thinly sliced   *Pepper and olive oil*
  cheese

Sift the flour and salt into a warm basin. Make a well in the centre and pour in the yeast which has been dissolved in a little of the warm milk and water. Fold the flour over the yeast with the fingers and keep folding it over until blended. Sprinkle a little flour over and round the dough, put a small blanket over the basin and leave in a warm place for the dough to rise (about 2 hours). The temperature should not be too hot or it will kill the yeast—30°C (85°F) is a good temperature and this may be achieved with a gas or electric oven with careful watching. (A wood or coke stove is ideal for the making of bread dough of course, for the basin may be left where the warmth will reach it.) When ready take the warm basin and stand it for a few minutes where the dough will be kneaded to avoid any sharp drop in temperature. Take out the dough, sprinkle a little flour on the table and knead gently with the fingers until it reaches the right consistency. This is felt immediately by a subtle change in the dough—it becomes light and elastic. Roll it out very thinly in two discs, place one on the bottom of a lightly oiled oven-proof dish, spread with the tomatoes, season with pepper, lay the anchovies on the tomatoes, then the cheese and sprinkle the oregano on top. Pour 1 dessertspoon of oil over all and then place the other disc on top just sealing the edges of the pie together with the fingers. Put in a hot oven (230°C or 450°F electric) for 20 minutes and eat it warm. It makes an excellent luncheon dish accompanied with a French salad in the winter for four people.

Parsley

A bed of parsley is almost indispensable, and it is looked on in much the same way as mint—a herb that we take for granted. There are many varieties of parsley, the best known being curled parsley (*Petroselinum crispum*), fern-leaved parsley (*P. crispum filicinum*), and Italian parsley (*P. crispum neapolitanum*). An old saying that parsley seed goes six times to the Devil and back before germinating reveals how slow it is in this respect! When preparing to put in the seeds in the spring or autumn they may be soaked in water for twelve hours before planting to hasten germination.

Parsley is a biennial, although it may be kept as a perennial by cutting the flower stalks when they appear. If it is in the right position, moist and sheltered with some sun during the day, and in fairly rich soil, some of the plants could be allowed to go to seed, when they will self-sow with no trouble. To make the most of your plants, always pick from the outside, allowing the new leaves to develop from the middle. As it is not very interesting when dried, we are fortunate in this country to be able to grow parsley and eat it fresh all the year round.

Parsley has been a valued medicinal herb extolled by writers since ancient times. Culpeper, quite a latter-day enthusiast comparatively, lists several different varieties, and has written nearly three pages on its virtues in treating all manner of diseases, particularly kidney and liver complaints. He also says it is a good salad herb.

There are many traditions associated with this herb, one being that if parsley is planted around the onion bed it will keep away the onion fly; another that if parsley is thrown into a fish pond, it will cure sick fish. There is probably a lot of truth in many of these old beliefs.

Today, as a culinary herb, parsley fulfils many requirements. It is excellent for garnishing, and adding, in a chopped-up form, to white sauce, scrambled egg and mashed potatoes. Many people do not know how rich in vitamins it is. When green vegetables are scarce, a tablespoonful of chopped parsley on each plate will help to make up the deficiency. Fried parsley with fish is really delicious. Parsley jelly and parsley ice are two excellent ways of using this herb. There is also that delicacy made with parsley which should accompany most grills—Green Butter.

Parsley · Jelly

Wash a big bunch of parsley (about 50 stalks). Put in a saucepan with enough water to cover, add the peel from a lemon and boil for about 1 hour. Strain the liquid into a basin and add the juice of 3 lemons. Measure, allowing a cup of sugar to every cup of liquid. Boil again until it begins to set. Drop in a little green colouring to improve the appearance. Put in jars, seal down and keep in a cool larder or refrigerator and eat it with chicken or fish. If it does not set, add a setting agent available from delicatessens.

Fried · Parsley

It is better not to wash the parsley, but if you do make sure it is absolutely dry before using. Break it up into sprigs and melt some butter in a frying pan. When the butter is hot and sizzling, but not black, put the sprigs in and let them fry quickly and crisply for about ½ minute or a little longer. Serve at once. The parsley should still be green, and not brown. Simple as this may sound, it takes a little practice which is well worth while.

Parsley · Ice

1 lemon	2 tablespoons finely chopped
300 ml (½ pint) water	parsley
½ cup sugar	1 tablespoon dry sherry and
1 stiffly beaten egg white	green colouring

A water-ice is sometimes eaten with the meat course. In hot weather it is particularly refreshing. Put the juice and finely grated rind of the lemon in a saucepan with the sugar and water. Bring to the boil and stir in the parsley. Simmer for 5 minutes. Cool, add the sherry and green colouring. Put in an ice tray and freeze. When forming crystals take out and mix into the beaten egg white. Return to the refrigerator to harden. It looks tempting when turned out onto a dish embedded in ice.

Rosemary

Rosemary (*Rosmarinus officinalis*), or "dew of the sea", is an aromatic shrub which was greatly favoured in Tudor days, not only for its appearance, but also for its usefulness in medicine and cooking. Shakespeare refers to it several times, Spenser called it "cheerful rosemarie", and Sir Thomas More says "I lette it run all over my garden walls". It does look effective against brick or stone, and the low-growing variety, *R. prostratus* is beautiful hanging in blue-flowered festoons over grey stones.

There are perhaps more legends wrapped around this freshly scented herb than any other. They are nearly all mystical or sacred. In Australia we have our own custom of wearing a sprig of rosemary for remembrance on Anzac Day.

There should be a sunny nook in every garden for a rosemary bush. Starred with pale blue flowers nearly all the year round and with its narrow leaves green on one side and grey underneath, it is most attractive. The whole plant, especially the seeds, contains natural oils. This makes it valuable to use in the making of pot-pourri, hair rinses, toilet waters and scented

rubbing lotions. Candied rosemary flowers, rosemary wine, rosemary honey and rosemary snow were once favoured confections. Today we know of it as a popular herb in Italian cooking, and the leaves used sparingly are excellent in certain food.

When we come upon a rosemary bush in the garden we may pause for a moment and remember some of the beautiful stories connected with it, and tell them to our children. It is not hard to imagine that fairies are supposed to use the flowers as their cradles.

There is the holy legend that during the flight into Egypt, the Virgin Mary threw her robe over a rosemary bush while she rested beside it. For ever afterwards the flowers which were previously white turned blue.

A picture called "The Legend of Rosemary", by Margaret W. Tarrant, shows Christ sitting on the ground while His Mother spreads His garments to dry on a rosemary bush. It is said this is the reason why the plant is so fragrant and "That bush forthgives, the faint, rare, sacred sweet of Him" (John Oxenham).

These and other sacred legends were probably the reasons why it was believed that carrying a sprig of rosemary was proof against all evil and that it should be carried by brides, as well as decorating churches with it on festive occasions.

Rosemary will grow from seed, but it is quicker and easier to propagate from semi-hardwood cuttings, taken with a heel if possible, at any time of the year—spring being the best time. It will flourish in a well-drained sunny position, sheltered from prevailing winds. Do not prune heavily, but if you are using and cutting it quite frequently once it is an established bush, this is all it needs.

Rosemary leaves with their fresh pungent flavour, give a delicious fragrance to food. As the leaves are thin and spiky, it is essential to cut them up finely. This is easily done by holding as many as you can together in your fingers, and then cutting them with the kitchen scissors into a container. When putting a sprig in to boil with pickled pork, corned beef or salted mutton it is not necessary to do this as the leaves are used to impart flavour.

Casserole · of · Beef
(A Mediterranean recipe)

2 kg (4 lb) roast of beef	1 doz. stoned black olives
250 g (½ lb) bacon cut into	1 dessertspoon rosemary,
fairly big pieces	finely chopped
1 cup of oil	1 wine glass red wine
2 cloves garlic	Salt and pepper
2 peeled tomatoes	

Cut the beef into thick rounds. Heat the oil in a fireproof dish on top of the stove, put in the meat and seal on both sides. Lower heat and add bacon, garlic and tomatoes. Simmer a little longer and add the rosemary, olives, salt, pepper and wine. Put the lid on the dish and cook in a slow oven for 2 hours.

Rosemary · Snow

One of the prettiest conceits from sophisticated Tudor days was Rosemary Snow. Imagine the gorgeously apparelled people helping themselves to this confection in much the same way as we each dip our toast into the Cheese Fondue today.

(In A Garden of Herbs, *by E. S. Rohde, from* A Book of Fruits and Flowers, *1653.)*

Take a quart [1.2 l] of thick Creame, and five or six whites of Eggs, a saucer full of Sugar finely beaten and as much Rosewater, beat them all together and always as it riseth take it out with a spoon, then take a loaf of Bread, cut away the crust, set it in a platter, and a great Rosemary bush in the middest of it, then lay your Snow with a Spoon upon the Rosemary, and so serve it.

Rosemary · Hair · Rinse

Pick a bunch of rosemary, cover it well with water and simmer it for ½ hour or more. A delicate fragrance and a tonic effect is given to the hair when given a final rinse with this preparation.

Roses

When talking of herbs and their uses, roses must not be overlooked. Roses were once of supreme importance in a garden; not only were they admired for their beauty, but they were considered so useful that instead of allowing them to fall or wither away, they were collected and used in many ways. There are countless old recipes involving roses: rose syrup and rose vinegar, oil of roses, rose water, rose-scented snuff, candied rose petals, rosehip syrup, rose honey, rose "cakes", sweet sachets, pot-pourri and rose-petal jam and jelly.

Roses have been loved by the human race for centuries, and the most scented of all, the damask rose, was said to have been brought from Damascus by the Crusaders. We still love roses for their beauty and fragrance, and new varieties are grown every year, but whatever one's personal choice may be, they are essential in a garden. When cut and brought indoors they are always enchanting, whether carefully arranged in fine china, or massed together in a cottage jug.

Immortal poems have been written about the rose. They have been exquisitely painted on canvas, parchment and old china, and deft fingers have woven them into emblems, and embroidered them on tapestries.

Redouté, a French artist of a century ago, made a complete study of them and painted very many varieties in loving detail. Excellent prints of them are available.

The eglantine of Chaucer and Shakespeare is the sweet briar rose, and it is the name Chaucer gives to his Prioress in *The Canterbury Tales*:

There was also a nun, a Prioress
Whose smile was simple, quiet, even coy.
The only oath she swore was, "By Saint Loy!"
And she was known as Sister Eglantine.

Constance Spry in her *Constance Spry Cookery Book* gives many recipes for using roses in cooking. She suggests that a spoonful or two of rose jam or jelly added to certain sweets gives them a delicious perfume and flavour.

Rose · Petal · Jam

(From Herbs and Herb Gardening, *by E. S. Rohde.)*

It is essential to use red, fragrant Roses. To fifty fully opened Roses allow 1000 ml (2 pints) of water, preferably clean rainwater or distilled water and 1.5 kg (3 lb) of the best preserving sugar. Boil the sugar and water till it candies a little. Add the juice of a small Lemon and the Rose petals. Stir well and bring to the boil. Put in a pat of butter to clear the scum and then simmer for quite an hour. It is necessary to stir very frequently, every five minutes or so, or the colour will be brown instead of red. Pour into pots and cover when cold.

I have made this recipe using ordinary tap water, and it really makes quite a large quantity. The consistency is more like a syrup than a thick jam. A setting agent can always be added at the end of cooking.

Rose · Vinegar

Fill a glass or crockery vessel with petals from scented roses and pour 600 ml (1 pint) of white vinegar over them. Cover and allow to infuse for 2 weeks, preferably in the sun. Strain, and use in the same way as tarragon vinegar.

Green · Salad · with · Rose · Petals

When ready to serve a lettuce salad, toss with a French dressing made with rose petal vinegar, add 1 tablespoon of rose petals from the tiny roses (or the smallest petals from scented roses) and mix again. Excellent for a luncheon with cold poultry.

Candied · Rose · Petals

Make sure the rose petals are not bruised and are thoroughly dry. Coat each one carefully with beaten white of egg applied with a small clean paint brush. Dust with castor sugar. Turn them over and repeat the process. Dry in the sun, occasionally turning them. When they are quite dry store in airtight jars between layers of grease-proof paper.

I can remember only pink ones being used; they were delicious on trifles with sugared violets and silver cashews nestling on whipped cream. They may also be used for decorating cakes.

Honey · of · Roses

(In A Garden of Herbs, *by E. S. Rohde, and from an old recipe by T. Tryon in* A Treatise of Cleanness in Meates, *1692.)*

Cut the white heels from Red Roses, take half a pound [250 g] of them and put them into a stone jar, and pour on them three pints [1800 ml] of boiling water. Stir well and let them stand twelve hours. Then press off the liquor, and when it has settled add to it five pounds [2.5 kg] of honey. Boil it well, and when it is of the consistence of a thick syrup it is ready to put away.

Pot-Pourri

If you have perfumed roses and lavender growing in the garden, as well as other fragrant flowers and leaved (scented-leaved geraniums, lemon-verbena, and sweet-smelling herb leaves), you have the main ingredients for making a pot-pourri.

Aromatic spices are blended with the flowery and leafy scents to give a warmly contrasting and interesting depth to the blend, while powdered orris root (the root or rhizome of the old Florentine iris) helps to "take up" the essential oils and to distribute them through the mixture while keeping it from becoming moist and mildewed.

Essential oils keep a pot-pourri fragrant for a much longer time than if they were not used at all. You can use two or three complementary but opposite-smelling oils, such as a sweet and a sharp perfume, with the addition of a lingering fragrance like musk or clove.

The following list is a guide to start with. . .later you will find that the blending of the oils for your own pot-pourri is very individual.

Sweet: Lavender, jasmine, rose, lily of the valley.

Sharp: Lemongrass, rosemary, petitgrain.

Lingering: Rose-geranium, musk, sandalwood, boronia, neroli, frangipani.

Flowers and leaves are gathered in dry weather early in the day before the sun has become too hot, then they are spread out to dry on racks or sheets of newspaper in a shady, airy place. (Scented leaves should be cut away from stems for quicker drying.) When crisp-dry, measure the flowers and leaves (large leaves should be crunched by hand into fairly small pieces) into an earthenware or glass container with a lid. To 4 cups of dried material you will need about 1 tablespoon (½ packet) of orris powder, 1 teaspoon each of the oils of your choice (say, lavender, petitgrain and sandalwood) and 1 teaspoon of ground cinnamon. Mix orris powder and cinnamon together, then add oils and amalgamate. Sprinkle this crumbly mixture over the dried flowers and leaves, stir well, close up and leave for 2–3 weeks, stirring occasionally. The blend is now ready for putting into one large decorative bowl, or into several smaller ones. Pieces of cinnamon bark, whole cloves, bay leaves and dried strips of orange or lemon peel may also go into a pot-pourri mixture.

As the spices retain their strength for years, dried flowers may be added from time to time. Rosemary and lavender flowers are especially good as they contain essential aromatic oils. When put into suitable bowls this makes a delightful gift.

Rose · Water

Nicholas Culpeper the seventeenth century herbalist says of rose water in *Culpeper's Complete Herbal*: "Red rose water is well known, and of a similar use on all occasions, and better than the damask rose-water, it is cooling, cordial, refreshing, quickening the weak and faint spirits, used either in meats or broths, to wash the temples, to smell at the nose, or to smell the sweet vapours out of a perfume pot, or cast into a hot fire-shovel."

There are many recipes for making rose water, but most of them are tedious and difficult with their instructions for distilling. The following recipe is quite simple. Some people use it in finger bowls, or put a little of it in a basin of water for guests to wash their hands.

Take 2 handfuls of scented red rose petals and put them in a jug or earthen pot. Pour over them 1200 ml (2 pints) of water and 250 g (½ lb) sugar. Let them steep for 1 hour. Take the water and roses and pour from one vessel into another until the water is scented with the flowers. Strain and keep in a cool place.

Sage

Sage (*Salvia officinalis*) is a popular perennial herb grown by many people today. It is one of the old favourites that has not been lost to us, probably because, for centuries, it was highly esteemed for its health-giving properties. "Why should a man die who has sage in his garden?" is an old proverb.

Sage prefers a light soil and a sunny position. When it has finished blooming cut off the flower stalks, and it will soon grow into a compact bush nearly one metre (three feet) high. Eventually it is wise to put in new plants, and this is easily done by breaking roots off from the old bush, or by sowing the seed when it is ripe.

According to the old writers, sage leaves are at their most beneficial in the spring, before the flower stalks begin to lengthen. It is also the best time for drying this herb.

The leaves are very pungent and slightly acrid, but they have a very pleasant flavour when cooked. Sage and onion stuffing with duck is well known, and leek tart flavoured with sage is delicious.

The leek (*Allium porrum*) is the emblem of Wales. It is also a "pot herb". Early plant lists indicate that "herbs for the pot" were the forerunners of many present day vegetables.

Leek pie with yeast pastry is an old favourite. The following recipe, Leek Tart with Sage, is delicious and simple to make. It has a very delicate flavour and is more palatable to those who find onions too strong. It goes very well with cold meat (lamb or mutton particularly) served with red currant jelly, or a sharp apple jelly. It is also excellent on its own with a French salad, and may be eaten either hot or cold. When preparing leeks for cooking, cut off the roots and leaves, leaving about two centimetres (one inch) of the green, and wash very well.

Leek · Tart · with · Sage

1 doz. leeks	*1 tablespoon finely chopped sage*
½ cup cream or top of milk	*leaves*
1 egg	*2 or 3 rashers of bacon*
1 tablespoon chopped parsley	*Salt and pepper*
	Short pastry

Cut the leeks into thin circles, put them in a saucepan with a little water and simmer gently until soft. Drain, and add the chopped herbs, the beaten egg and the cream, mixing it all together. Adjust seasoning.

Line a lightly floured pie dish with thinly rolled short pastry. Prick it well, and spoon in the leek mixture. Cut the bacon into small squares (after removing the rind) and arrange on top of the tart. Bake in a medium to hot oven for about 20 minutes.

The short pastry I make is a recipe from my husband's family, and known as Emily's Pastry. Hers was so light that it almost blew away, and yet it was rich and full of flavour.

Emily's · Pastry

1 good cup self-raising flour
60 g (2 oz) butter
½ cup cold water with a little
    lemon juice added

Pinch salt (and a pinch of
    sugar when using for sweets)

Sift dry ingredients. Rub butter and flour together with finger-tips. Add water gradually and mix lightly with a knife. Roll lightly. Place in a fairly hot oven for 20 minutes. Do not brown too quickly. Always open and close oven door very gently— never bang.

Cheese flavoured with sage has been favoured by country people for years. Welsh rarebit made with beer and flavoured with sage makes a particularly appetizing Sunday night meal.

Welsh · Rarebit · with · Sage

250 g (½ lb) grated tasty
    cheese
1 dessertspoon finely chopped
    sage leaves

1 cup beer
Salt, pepper, ½ teaspoon
    mustard

Warm the beer in a saucepan, and gradually add the cheese, then the sage, salt, pepper and mustard. Stir well until the cheese has melted. Serve hot with triangles of hot buttered toast.

Sage · and · Onion · Stuffing
(From Mrs Beeton's Poultry and Game.)

Take 4 large onions, 10 sage leaves, 125 g (¼ lb) of breadcrumbs, 40 g (1½ oz) of butter, salt and pepper to taste, and 1 egg.

Peel the onions, put them into boiling water, let them simmer for 5 minutes or rather longer, and, just before they are taken out, put in the sage leaves for a minute or two to take off their rawness. Chop both these very fine, add the bread, seasoning, and butter, and work the whole together with the yolk of an egg, when the stuffing will be ready for use. If should be rather highly seasoned, and the sage leaves should be very finely chopped. Many cooks do not parboil the onions in the manner just stated, but merely use them raw, but the stuffing then is not nearly so mild, and, to many tastes, its strong flavour would be very objectionable. When made for goose, a portion of the liver of the bird, simmered for a few minutes and very finely minced, is frequently added to this stuffing; and where economy is studied, the egg and butter may be omitted.

This should be sufficient for 1 goose, or a pair of ducks.

Savory

Summer savory (*Satureia hortensis*) and winter savory (*S. montana*) are the two popular varieties of this genus for use in cooking. Seed of the summer savory, which is an annual, is sown in the spring, the plant growing to about half a metre (one and a half feet) high. Winter savory, a perennial, may be grown from seed also, but it is usually more satisfactory to divide the roots in the spring, when it will grow rapidly into a bushy shrub a little over thirty centimetres (twelve inches) high. A pleasing idea would be to plant a dwarf hedge of winter savory, as in Tudor days. It also makes an attractive plant for herbaceous borders. Grow both varieties of savory in light soil in the sun.

At first glance the savories resemble thyme; however, on closer inspection, you will see that the leaves are longer and quite narrow. Like thyme the leaves are pungent, but with a hot peppery flavour. It is said that rubbing a leaf on a bee sting will relieve the pain.

Both summer savory and winter savory have been used for many years on the Continent in meat and fish dishes (it is supposed to be especially good with trout), in stuffings, and boiled with beans as mint is with peas. A Tudor custom was to mix dried savory with breadcrumbs giving a "quicker relish" to crumbed fish or meat.

Winter savory is a well-contented habitué of the window trough. Do not plant it, however, with parsley or chives as it may take over the whole container.

Savory · Stuffing · for · Fish

1 cup soft breadcrumbs	60 g (2 oz) butter
Grated rind and juice of 1	1 tablespoon finely chopped
lemon	onion
1 dessertspoon finely chopped	1 egg
savory	Salt and pepper

Soften the butter in a frying pan and gently fry the onion without browning. Add to the other ingredients in a bowl, binding the mixture with the egg. 1 doz. oysters, or 1 cup shelled prawns may be added with advantage to the stuffing.

Fried · Tripe · and · Winter Savory

750 g (1½ lb) tripe	1 tablespoon fresh or
1 chopped white onion	1 dessertspoon dried savory
1½ cups oil	1 tin or 250 g (½ lb) fresh
2 thinly sliced cloves of garlic	mushrooms
	Flour

Simmer the tripe for about an hour. Drain in a colander, allowing the cold tap to run over it. Fry the onion and garlic in the oil until soft. Cut the tripe into cubes, roll in flour and add to the onion and garlic. Fry until golden, adding more oil if necessary. Put in a fireproof dish, add the mushrooms, savory and 300 ml (½ pint) of stock. Cover and simmer in a slow oven for 1 hour. Even people who don't care for tripe, usually like it this way.

Baked · Fish · with · Cider

1 kg (2 lb) fish fillets	3 finely sliced shallots
1 tablespoon finely chopped	1 breakfast cup cider
savory	Soft breadcrumbs and butter
2 peeled and cored apples cut	
into wedges	

Roll the fillets in flour and put them in a buttered fireproof dish with the apple, savory and shallots. Season with salt and freshly ground pepper. Pour the cider in slowly and carefully. Top with breadcrumbs which have been lightly fried in butter. Bake in a moderate oven for about 20 minutes. The fragrance of apple and cider united with spicy savory combines well with fish.

Scented-Leaved Geraniums

Scented geraniums are a valuable addition to the herb garden, not only because their leaves impart subtle depths of perfume to pot-pourri, but also because they may be used to flavour certain foods. All geranium leaves have a rather pungent quality. This is much more marked in some kinds than in others, and there are a number of varieties whose leaves are redolent of familiar scents which brings to mind the interesting fact that plant scents have their own tones and variations, just as in music and colour.

There seems to be an essential element which makes some plants smell of apples, lemons, roses and so on. The apple-scented geranium, *Pelargonium odoratissimum*, for instance, smells strongly of Granny Smith apples even when lightly brushed in passing. It is a delicate spreading plant, with round, green leaves and fragile, white flowers, valuable for borders or in the rockery.

The nutmeg-scented geranium, *P. fragrans*, at first glance is rather similar, but it is of more upright growth, and when the ruffled leaves are crushed the spicy scent reminds one of freshly ground nutmegs. The rose-scented geranium, from which the well-known oil of geranium is extracted, is said to be *P. capitatum*, although there is another variety known as attar-of-roses, or *P. graveolens*, which is thought by many to be the rose geranium, its leaves having much the same elusive perfume. The variety Lady Plymouth is also rose scented, and the leaves are variegated green and gold.

The lemon-scented geranium, *P. limonium*, has leaves smelling of lemons and something more, which is probably verbena, and this may be the reason why it is often called "lemon-scented verbena". The crisp leaves are long, very serrated and decorative, and the flowers, a delicate shade of pinky-mauve, are small and single. One or two leaves are often used to flavour jellies, custards, rice puddings and sponge cakes; when dried they give their warm yet lemony fragrance to pot-pourri, and the dried flowers, too, impart their fragrance and colour. The leaves of this variety are excellent for use in flower arrangements.

Some other varieties smelling of lemons are *P. asperium*, which has similar leaves to the lemon-scented, except that they are very sticky. The decorative *P. crispum variegata* looks like a miniature cypress tree and the lemon-scented leaves are small, curly and variegated.

Many people consider that *P. tomentosum* is the most fascinating variety of the scented-leaved geraniums. The peppermint-scented leaves are large and velvety, of a clear-green colour, delightfully described by Gertrude Jekyll to be "thick as a fairy's blanket, soft as a vicuna robe". There are recipes for using the leaves to make peppermint jelly, and if you wish to follow a Greek custom flavour apple jelly by putting them, as well as other sweet-scented geranium leaves (only two or three at a time), into the preserving pan during the last five minutes of cooking.

Take them out before sealing the jelly in pots, but a fresh leaf may be put in for decoration and flavour. In flower arrangements the peppermint-scented leaves lend contrast in texture and form against other leaves and as a soft foil for flowers; red roses, nestling against the tender green of these leaves, are particularly enchanting. The plant itself is rampant and sprawling, and likes room to grow; the small white flowers, as is often the case with sweet-scented geraniums, are insignificant.

An interesting scented variety is the coconut-scented *P. enossularoides*, which has crimson flowers and leaves similar to the apple-scented geranium. Another is *P. abrotanifolium*, sometimes known as southernwood, the scent of the leaves being exactly like that of southernwood or lad's love.

Clorinda is sweetly named and lovely to look at with eucalyptus-scented leaves of brightish-green and single pelargonium-like flowers of rich cyclamen. *P. denticulatum* has very cut and fragile leaves, which are sticky and smell warm and spicy. It has mauve flowers. Fair Helen or Fair Ellen is an old favourite with large, pungent oak leaves and magenta flowers. Besides the ones mentioned here there are many more, an almost bewildering variety, and all a lesson in scent perception.

Last but not least in this chapter of geraniums is the little herb Robert, or Geranium Robert, as it is sometimes called. It is an annual with a delicate trailing habit, small round leaves and single deep pink flowers; today it makes a delightful herbaceous plant, but it was once valued in herbal therapy for its styptic qualities.

All the scented-leaved geraniums may be dried and used in pot-pourri except the sticky varieties. It is important to dry the peppermint-scented leaves carefully as they are inclined to retain moisture and to mildew. Spread them out on paper in warm, dry weather when there is no humidity in the air. Constance Spry suggests that scented geranium leaves can improve the flavour of a cake.

Attar · of · Roses · Sponge

4 eggs	*Rose-geranium leaves*
170 g (6 oz) sugar	*1 level tablespoon butter*
1 1/4 cups self-raising flour	*4 tablespoons hot water*
2 level tablespoons cornflour	*Pinch salt*

Separate the egg whites and beat until stiff, gradually add the sugar and beat until it is dissolved, then gently mix in the egg yolks. Sift the flour, cornflour and salt 3 times, lightly fold it into the cake mixture, have the butter melted and the hot water ready and fold in carefully. Grease and lightly flour two 20 cm (8 inch) cake tins, lay rose-geranium leaves on the bottom of the tins and pour in the cake mixture. Bake in a fairly hot oven (200°C or 400°F electric) on the bottom shelf for 20 minutes. Turn out on a wire tray and leave to cool. The geranium leaves may be left on the bottom of the cake until ready for filling, allowing the flavour to penetrate. Fill the sponge with cream and sift a little icing sugar on the top. The perfume from the geranium leaves will linger, giving the cake a subtle fragrance.

Lemon-Scented · Baked · Custard

3 eggs	*1 medium-sized lemon-scented*
600 ml (1 pint) milk	*geranium leaf*
2 tablespoons sugar	*A little butter*

Break the eggs into a fireproof dish, add the sugar and beat together with a fork. Pour the milk gradually on the eggs, beating all the time. Dot with butter and place the geranium leaf in the centre of the custard. Put the dish in a pan containing about an inch of cold water and cook in a medium oven until the custard is set, about ¾ hour. The geranium leaf gently imparts its lemony aroma to the custard—a plain rice pudding may be flavoured in the same way.

Peppermint · Jelly

4 lemons
1 cup sugar
1 pint very hot water
3 dessertspoons gelatine

Green colouring or crème de
menthe
Peppermint-scented geranium
leaves

Pick and wash a bunch of peppermint-scented geranium leaves, put them in a basin and bruise with a spoon. Squeeze the lemons and pour the juice on the geranium leaves, add the sugar. Cover the basin and leave for at least 2 hours. Strain the liquid through a sieve, pressing all moisture out of the leaves. Dissolve the gelatine in a little of the hot water, pour the rest of the water and dissolved gelatine into the peppermint-scented liquid. Add a tablespoon of crème de menthe if you wish, or a few drops of green colouring, and stir well. Pour the jelly into a dish and decorate the centre with a peppermint-scented geranium leaf. Leave to set.

Baked · Apples · with · Geranium Leaves

4 green cooking apples
1 tablespoon apple jelly

4 apple-scented geranium leaves
A little butter

Wash the apples, cut a little of the peel away from the top and core (a clean wooden "dolly" clothes peg is most efficient). Put a little butter into the hollows in the apples, add 1 teaspoon of apple jelly to each apple and top with an apple-scented geranium leaf. Stand the apples in a little water in a fireproof dish and bake in a medium to hot oven until just soft. Pour the liquid from the dish into a saucepan, add 1 tablespoon of sugar and boil for a few minutes, add a little red colouring and pour the syrup over the apples. Eat them hot with thick cream, and the geranium leaves, which become crisp, are edible too.

Tarragon

Tarragon (*Artemisia dracunculus*) is a herb renowned for its distinctive aromatic flavour. The most fragrant culinary variety, known as French or "true" tarragon, does not set seed, while the inferior Russian tarragon does. In this country there has been much controversy as to whether there is any true tarragon here at all.

The only way to have French tarragon in the garden is to plant a root of it, and even then, perhaps, connoisseurs, who have travelled widely, will be doubtful about whether it is the real thing. The climatic and soil conditions often affect the characteristic flavour of a plant to a greater or lesser degree. The dried leaves are more aromatic than the fresh, although a bite into the green tartness will show the flavour pungent enough. Grow the plant in light, rather poor soil in a warm position, allowing it to absorb as much sunlight as possible so that it will then have the opportunity of showing what may be achieved in the way of flavour.

Poultry and fish are flavoured with tarragon, and a few of the fresh leaves are delicious in a cucumber salad. It is also the correct herb to use in tartare sauce.

Tarragon vinegar is quickly made. Pack a glass jar with tarragon leaves, pour white vinegar over, cover and infuse for two weeks. Strain and pour into bottles. A fresh branch of tarragon put into the bottle not only adds strength to the vinegar, but looks effective.

Some of the Artemisia family, to which tarragon belongs, are not culinary herbs, but were once used in medicine, and in the household. They were grown in every cottage garden. It is not out of place therefore to mention them here. We know them by their homely old names of lad's love, dusty miller and old woman.

Southernwood (A. abrotanum), sometimes called old man or lad's love, is a metre (three foot) high ornamental shrub with the most delicate grey-green foliage. Bitter-sweet describes the scent and flavour of this herb. It is very aromatic with a slight touch of ether about it. Perhaps this is why it was once a remedy for insomnia!

Wormwood (A. absinthum) is also one of the bitter herbs, and is used in the making of absinthe. It was highly valued for its medicinal qualities and was also strewn amongst clothes to keep away moths. "It is a very noble bitter, and succeeds in procuring an appetite", observes Culpeper. It is said to be "Dian's bud" which Oberon used to waken Titania in A Midsummer Night's Dream.

Sea wormwood (A. stelleriana), or old woman, is yet another of this family, a much lower-growing variety and not so aromatic, and as its botanical name indicates, it likes sandy soil.

Sauce · Tartare

1 egg yolk	1 dessertspoon chopped olives
1/2 cup olive oil	1 dessertspoon chopped tarragon
1 tablespoon tarragon vinegar	A little mustard, salt and
1 teaspoon chopped capers	pepper
(optional)	

Put the egg yolk into a basin with the mustard, salt and pepper. Drop the oil onto this gradually, stirring well all the time until the mixture is smooth and thick. Beat in the vinegar carefully, add the olives, tarragon and capers. Serve with fish.

Chicken · Supreme · with · Peaches

1 fowl	4 ripe peaches
2 tablespoons butter	2 tablespoons finely chopped
1 1/2 tablespoons flour	tarragon
1 egg	Salt and pepper
1/2 cup thick cream	

Put the fowl on a wire sieve in a large saucepan and steam it gently until it is tender. Lift out, cut into pieces and arrange on a large plate. Keep it warm. Melt the butter, add the flour, stirring until it is well blended. Gradually add 450 ml (3/4 pint) of stock in which the chicken was cooked and stir until it thickens. Adjust seasoning. Beat the egg and cream together and pour into the sauce. Stir for 1/2 minute, remove from the stove, and mask the chicken with it. Peel and cut the peaches into halves, poach gently, drain and arrange around the chicken. Sprinkle with tarragon and serve very hot. If fresh peaches are not available, the best tinned peaches will do.

Crab · and · Avocado · Mould

2 cups crabmeat	1 1/2 tablespoons gelatine
2 avocados peeled and diced	1 tablespoon chopped tarragon
1 cup diced celery	Salt and pepper
1 tin tomato soup	

Mix the crabmeat, avocado, tarragon and celery together, adjust seasoning. Soak the gelatine in 1/2 cup of heated tomato soup for 5 minutes then stir it slowly into the remainder of the soup. Pour this over the crabmeat mixture and set it in a mould. When firm, turn it out on a bed of watercress or finely shredded lettuce surrounded by slices of lemon.

Thyme

As there are numerous varieties of thyme, it may become a fascinating hobby for the interested gardener to collect as many different kinds as possible, not only for the herb garden, but also for rockeries and to cover inhospitable ground.

Thyme is truly the enchanted herb. E. S. Rohde declares that "wild thyme has always been a favourite with fairies" and she goes on to give an old recipe "To enable one to see the Fairies". It is directed that the "vial glasse in which the liquid is made must first be washed with rose-water and marygolde water", and the flowers gathered towards the east from the side of a fairy throne. Indulgent fancy though it may be, it is the small, scented plants which creep so joyfully over the ground with their softly hued flowers, the graceful foxgloves and campanulas that rise in spires against a green garden, and the native *Grevillea rosmarinifolia* with its delicate rose and cream spider flowers, that entrance all who see them, and make us feel that perhaps in some gardens Ariel may be lurking and softly singing: "Where the bee sucks, there suck I."

Edna Walling delights us by writing: "Luxuries of luxuries! I've been lying on my own thyme lawn, there was just enough room to turn over without landing on to the surrounding rock plants. You haven't lived if you have not lain flat on your middle on a thyme lawn."

Thyme grows wild in Europe, from the mountains of Greece to the rolling downs of England and in parts of Asia and Africa. Bees have always loved this herb, and honey made from thyme is the most delicious and fragrant of all. Thyme was always planted near the bee-hives and the hives were also rubbed with it.

Thyme is very easy to grow; propagate by root division, or strike cuttings in sand in late winter; grow the plants in light, well-drained soil in a sunny position and you will be rewarded by a spreading, thickly foliaged little plant in a very short time.

In spring and summer the scented flowers of the different varieties shade from reddish purple through soft lilac and pink to white. Although each variety has its own individuality of perfume, flavour and form, they are all aromatic. The volatile oil from this herb, thymol, is extracted and used in industry. In Roman times this herb was a remedy for melancholy, and today a tea made from the leaves is regarded as being invigorating and refreshing.

There are a great number of different thymes, the following varieties being the most easily obtainable at present.

Garden thyme (*Thymus vulgaris*) is the species most often used in flavouring. It is a particularly savoury herb, growing into a shrubby plant about thirty centimetres (one foot) high, with pale, creamy-pink flowers in spring. It dries very successfully; harvest the branches just before the plant flowers and hang up in a shady place for two or three weeks. Rub the dry leaves off the brittle stalks and store in airtight glass jars. The pungency of your own dried thyme surpasses that of any bought kind.

Lemon thyme (*T. citriodorus*) is aptly named, having a delicious lemon scent overlaying the typical thymy flavour. The leaves are softer and rounder than garden thyme, and are therefore more satisfactory to use in cooking when picking sprays straight from the garden; it is also valuable when dried. The plant grows to a height of thirty centimetres (twelve inches) and has fragrant pink flowers in spring and all through the summer, the colour of a moss-rose. It is a hue difficult to describe because it is not the pink we know today, nor is it mauve, but a soft combination of both, delicate, and restful to the eyes.

Variegated thyme (*T. citriodorus variegatus*) has green leaves with white or gold variegation and a definite lemon scent also. It may be used both as an ornamental plant and in cooking; it grows to thirty centimetres (twelve inches) high and has pink flowers.

Caraway thyme (*T. herba-barona*) has a creeping habit and pink flowers. It has an unmistakable scent, redolent of caraway, and may be used in the kitchen to give a subtle flavour to certain food. The leaves stripped from the stalk give a fresh and piquant flavour to sandwiches cut very thinly and spread first with smooth scrambled egg.

T. nitidus is a fascinating little plant particularly suitable for rocky niches and those small spaces that should be left when flagging a terrace. It grows up into a little green hillock, looking rather like a spreading miniature bonsai tree, and in summer it is powdered with pale, mauve-tinted flowers.

T. pauciflorus is a strong-growing carpeting thyme with green foliage and soft pink flowers; it is excellent for rockeries and borders.

T. serpyllum is reputed to be Shakespeare's "wild thyme", and because of its magic associations is a magic herb; Culpeper calls it "Mother of thyme".

It has a vigorous creeping habit, is very fragrant and covered with bright pink flowers in summer. It looks most attractive growing around the sundial in a herb garden. This is the variety which is recommended for use in a thyme lawn, and for making a fragrant garden seat by putting earth where you desire your scented seat to be, and then planting the thyme in the early spring to form a dense mat, which it does very quickly.

T. serpyllum coccineous is very similar to the above but with a greater profusion of flowers.

T. serpyllum lanuginosus has tiny woolly leaves, delicately scented. It forms a thick, grey carpet which is most effective for a rockery. It grows nicely on top of a herb-garden wall where it will fall in thin silver strands over the golden stones.

T. serpyllum albus is a carpeting thyme with green foliage and drifts of white flowers in the spring.

Westmoreland thyme grows to two feet with soft mauve flowers. It could be described as Edna Walling's own. She mentions it many times in her books, as for instance: "One of the most perfect of all edging plants is the Westmoreland thyme, a variety of *T. serpyllum* which is mid-way between *T. vulgaris*, the common culinary thyme (an excellent carpeting and edging plant by the way) and the ground clinging *T. serpyllum* known variously as Shepherd's thyme and Mother of thyme."

There are many well-known stuffing and force-meat recipes employing thyme and a sniff of a spray of it will immediately make you think of roast chicken and turkey. The green leaves may be stripped from the stalks and used in place of dried thyme for a change, but the aroma of this herb is more penetrating when dried.

Thyme · Stuffing · for · Poultry

1 cup of white breadcrumbs	Salt and freshly ground pepper
60 g (2 oz) butter	1 tablespoon thyme
1 tablespoon finely chopped	1 dessertspoon chopped parsley
onion	1 dessertspoon chopped
Grated rind and juice of 1	marjoram
lemon	1 egg

Soften the onion in a frying pan in the butter without browning. Put all the ingredients in a bowl binding them together with the egg.

Rabbit · Cooked · in · Milk

1 rabbit	600 ml (1 pint) milk
2 tablespoons flour	Salt and pepper
125 g (4 oz) butter or 1 small	1 tablespoon dried thyme or 2
cup of oil	tablespoons fresh chopped
2 finely chopped onions	thyme

Cut the rabbit into pieces and roll in the flour. Heat the butter or oil and gently fry the floured rabbit on both sides. Put the rabbit, onions and thyme in layers in a fireproof dish, seasoning as you go with salt and pepper. Pour in 600 ml (1 pint) of milk, cover the dish and cook in a moderately slow oven for 2 hours.

We have been enjoying this recipe ever since the war years when meat was rationed and rabbit was very popular and cooked in many different ways.

Savoury · Meat · Loaf

250 g (½ lb) minced bacon	2 teaspoons dried thyme or 1
500 g (1 lb) minced steak	tablespoon fresh chopped
½ cup white breadcrumbs	thyme
1 chopped onion	½ cup milk
1 egg	Salt and pepper

Put the minced steak and bacon into a bowl and add the breadcrumbs, onion, thyme, salt and pepper. Work it well together with a fork, add the milk and the egg, blending the whole mixture. Turn it into a loaf tin and bake in a moderate oven for 1 hour.

It would be foolish in a book of this size to try to discuss all the medicinal herbs and their uses. The few that have been mentioned are well known for their health-giving qualities.

A herbal tea, or tisane, is an infusion of boiling water and herbs, either fresh or dried, and is usually taken after dinner or before going to bed, with a little lemon and honey added. These teas are more widely known in other countries than in Australia. They are both pleasant to drink and beneficial, often being a remedy for a mild indisposition. Many people assert that taking them over a long period builds up a resistance to a number of illnesses.

In England, particularly in the country, herbal teas still retain their popularity; in France it is the custom to have a tisane on retiring; in America a famous beauty salon serves chamomile tea to help clear the complexion and to soothe the nerves, and the Chinese have known the value of herbal teas for hundreds of years.

It is said that at the end of the day, after the exacting demands of our present life, which distracts the mind and tires the body, a herbal tea unites the spirit and the body again in harmony with oneself and the universe. An infusion of the flower-heads of German chamomile is recommended to bring about this tranquil sensation of well-being.

Some well-known herbal teas are those made of lime-flowers, orange flowers, lemon-scented verbena leaves, hyssop flowers, bergamot leaves and sage leaves, the last-named herb having once had the reputation of delaying old age. Dried nettle tea is a natural source of iron; rosemary tea is supposed to stimulate the memory; peppermint tea, if taken regularly, helps to ward off colds; mint, lemon-thyme and balm tea in the summer are all refreshing and invigorating, and angelica tea helps digestion.

There are numerous varieties of the chamomile daisy growing in many gardens and superficially they look alike, with their finely cut, fern-like leaves and tiny, white-and-gold daisy flower-heads, but there are differences in appearance and their uses are not the same. It is interesting also to note the different botanical headings under which they are known. The most usual kind found in gardens is the old feverfew or febrifuge, *Chrysanthemum parthenium*, and is not used very much today in herbal teas. It was once considered a cure for headaches. Culpeper says with some asperity, "and if any grumble because they cannot get the herb in winter, tell them, if they please, they may make a syrup of it in summer".

Both the English chamomile (*Anthemis nobilis*), a perennial, and the German chamomile (*Matricaria chamomilla*), an annual, are widely used in herbal

teas. There seems to be some difference of opinion among herbal writers as to which is the "true" chamomile, and which has the most efficacy. "May-then" was the old Saxon name for English chamomile, and the Spaniards call it "manzilla", meaning little apple. A Spanish wine, flavoured with chamomile, is known by the same name; this is also the variety recommended for a chamomile lawn. For tea, only the dried flower-heads are used, and these should be gathered early in the morning and spread out to dry on paper in a cool, airy place; when dry put the fragrant heads in clean dry screwtop jars.

German chamomile grows to a height of thirty centimetres (twelve inches) and should be planted in a plot by itself and allowed to self-sow as the seed is rather difficult to collect. When the white-and-gold flowers are massed together like this they make a brave show. Harvest and dry the flower-heads in the same way as English chamomile. By the way, there is an old saying that where chamomile grows the plants in the garden will be healthier.

Chamomile · Tea   (1   Cup)

Measure 1 cup of water into an enamel saucepan and bring to the boil, sprinkle 1 teaspoon of dried chamomile heads into the water, put on the lid and boil for ½ minute. Remove from the stove and leave the lid on for a little longer so that the valuable essence is not lost. Strain into a cup, flavour with a little lemon juice and sweeten with honey if you wish. It is delicious.

Peppermint · Tea   (2   or   3   Cups)

The true Mitcham peppermint (*Mentha piperita officinalis*) is used for this tea and is recommended to take as a prevention against colds. The character of this mint's aroma is warmly pungent, while the other mints have a lighter, more piercing quality. Like the rest of the mint family, peppermint prefers a fairly moist position and room to spread. Snails love this particular mint so be on guard against these marauders. Tea is made from either the fresh or dried leaves: if using fresh leaves, pick a handful from the garden and put them in a crockery teapot, preferably one kept for this purpose, as there is then no taint from ordinary tea present, pour boiling water on to the leaves, cover and leave to infuse for 5 minutes. Sweeten with honey and flavour with lemon. If using the dried leaves, pick a bundle of stalks in the morning after the dew has gone and spread out to dry. When ready strip the leaves from the stems and put in airtight jars.

Mint · Teas

Dried or fresh mint may be used, and made in the same way as Peppermint Tea.

Sparkling · Mint · Tea

(From The Coronation Cookery Book, *compiled by the Country Women's Association of* N.S.W.)

3.6 l (3 quarts) strong tea   *450 ml (³/4 pint) lemon juice*
1.8 l (1¹/2 quarts) soda water   *Mint and ice*
3 cups castor sugar

Make tea in the usual way, allow 4 teaspoons tea to 1.2 l (a quart) of boiling water. Infuse and then strain, add sugar, stand it until cool. Stir in lemon juice to tea, add soda and serve in tall glass jug with a lump of ice. Place sprigs of mint on rim of glass and in the jug. A few berries, green grapes, or a slice of lemon and orange may be added to each jug. This quantity makes 6 l (1¼ gallons), suitable for a large party.

This is a refreshing drink to serve at a tennis party.

Nettle · Tea

Nettle (*Urtica dioica*), the "wergulu" of early Saxon writings was with "maythen", chervil and fennel one of the sacred herbs of those days. It contains iron and protein, and a tisane made of the dried leaves infused in the same way as peppermint tea, helps a cold. The green beverage has a rich, smooth flavour tasting of all the good green things which come from the earth, and in my opinion is best on its own without lemon and honey.

Rosemary · Tea

Pick a fresh sprig of rosemary from the garden and put it in a cup, pour boiling water over, stand a saucer on the top to keep in the fumes and leave to infuse for 5 minutes. If making more than 1 cup, pick several sprigs and make the tea in a crockery teapot.

Angelica · Tea

Pick a few fresh angelica leaves and put them in a crockery teapot; pour boiling water on to them, cover and leave to infuse for 5 minutes.

Index

Allium sativus. *See* Garlic
Allium schoenoprasum. *See* Chives
Anchusa, 11
Anethum. *See* Dill
Angelica, 11, 27–28
    tea, 107
Anthemis nobilis. *See* Chamomile
Anthriscus cerefolium. *See* Chervil
Applemint, 67
Apples, baked, with geranium leaves, 93
Aromatic herb baths, 23, 42, 62
Artemisia. *See* Tarragon
Attar-of-roses sponge cake, 92

Balm, 11, 16, 29–31
    and marshmallow custard, 31
    and orange frosted, 31
    dressing for orange salad, 31
Bananas and mint, fried, 69
Basil, 11, 16, 32–34
    vinegar, 33
Bath, herbs for, 23, 42, 62
Bay leaves, 35–36
Beef casserole with herbs, 78
Bergamot, 11, 37–39
    salad, 39
    sauce, 39
Bergamot mint, 68
Borage, 11, 16, 40–42
Borago officinalis. *See* Borage
Bouquet of herbs, 35, 63

Cabbage, meat-stuffed, with herbs, 36
Candles, scented, 24
Chamomile, 11, 12, 13
    tea, 106
Chervil, 11, 16, 42–44
Chicken supreme with peaches, 96

Chicory, 11, 45–46
    and poached eggs, 46
    salad, 46
Chives, 11, 16, 46–49
Cichorium intybus. *See* Chicory
Clove orange, 20
Clove-pinks, 12
Coathanger, scented, 23
Coleslaw with dill, 53
Containers for indoor herb-
    growing, 16, 17
Coriander, 11, 49–51
Coriandrum. *See* Coriander
Cosmetic (herb) baths, 23, 42, 62
Cottage pie with herbs, 64
Crab and avocado mould, 96
Cream cheese and chives, 47
Crystallized flowers, 41
Cucumber, creamed, 48
Custard, caramel, 42
    lemon-scented baked, 92

Dill, 11, 51–53
Drying of herbs, 13–14

Egg tart, minted, 69
Eggs and chicory, 46
Emily's pastry, 86

Fennel, 11, 16, 54–56
    cream sauce, 55
    with sausage, 56
Fish, baked, with cider, 89
    pie, with herbs, 49
Foeniculum vulgare. *See* Fennel
Foxglove, 12
French dressing, 34
    See also Salad dressing

Garlic, 56–59
Geraniums, scented-leaf, 12, 16, 89–93
  for sweet bags, 22

Haricot beans with tomatoes and
    herbs, 44
Heliotrope, 12
Herb-growing, 11–14, 16–17
  See also individual herbs
Herbal teas, 104–107
Hollyhocks, 12
Honey of roses, 82
Honey soap, 24
Honeysuckle, 12
Hyssop, 11

Jasmine, 12

Ladder herb-gardens, 6
Lamb's fry with basil, 34
Laurus nobilis. See Bay leaves
Lavandula. See Lavender
Lavender, 11, 12, 16, 59–63
  bags, 22
  sugar, 62
  vinegar, 62
  water, 62
Lawns, herb, 12, 13
Leek tart with sage, 85
Lovage, 11

Marjoram, 11, 16, 63–66
  vinegar, 66
  See also Oregano
Marmalade, coriander-flavoured, 51
Meat loaf, savoury, 101
Melissa officinalis. See Balm
Mentha. See Mint
Menthol, 68
Mint, 11, 16, 67–70
  jelly, 70
  julep, 69
  leaves, crystallized, 70
  sauce, 68
  teas, 107
Minted egg tart, 69
Monarda didyma. See Bergamot

Nettle tea, 107
Note-paper, scented, 24

Ocimum. See Basil
Orange, clove, 20
Oregano, 11, 16, 71–73
Origanum. See Marjoram
Orris root, 20
Oswego tea, 39

Parsley, 16, 74–76
  fried, 75
  ice, 76
  jelly, 75
Pastry, Emily's, 86
Pathways, herb, 12
Pears, glazed, 28
Pelargonium. See Geraniums
Pennyroyal, 11, 12, 16
  See also Mint
Peppermint, 68
  jelly, 93
  tea, 106
Petroselinum. See Parsley
Pineapple cocktail, 70
Pizza pie, 72
Planting of herbs, in pots, 16
  in a wheel or ladder, 6
  See also individual herbs
Pomander ball, 20
Pork sausages with apple and
    bergamot, 38
Pot-pourri, 20, 82
Potato pie and marjoram, 66
Potato soup with chervil, 44
Primroses, 12

Rabbit cooked in milk, with thyme, 101
Rhubarb and angelica leaves, 29
Rice salad with basil, 34
Rosemary, 11, 12, 16, 23, 76–79
  hair rinse, 79
  rubbing lotion, 23
  snow, 79
  tea, 107
Rose-petal jam, 81
Rose petals, candied, 81

Rose vinegar, 81
Rose water, 83
Roses, 12, 79–83
  See also Rose petals
Rubbing lotion, 23
Rue, 11, 12

Sage, 11, 16, 84–87
  and onion stuffing, 86
Salad, chicory, 46
  green, with rose petals, 81
Salad dressing, balm, 31
  with basil, 33, 34
Salvia. *See* Sage
Sandwiches, herb, 5, 63, 69
Santolina, 62
Santureia. *See* Savory
Sauce tartare, 96
Sausage, fennel-seed, 56
Sausages, in cider, 58
  with apple and bergamot, 38
Savory, 11, 16, 87–89
  stuffing for fish, 88
Scallops with dill, 53
Scones, herb, 65
Soap, honey, 24
Soil mixtures for herbs, 17
  See also individual herbs
Southernwood, 95
Spaghetti and oregano, 72
Spearmint, 67
Sponge cake, attar-of-roses, 92

Steak, burning, 66
  casserole with bay leaves and pickled
    walnuts, 36
  grilled with oregano, 72
  kebabs, 72
  rolls, stuffed, 59
Sugar, lavender, 62
Sweet bags, 22

Tarragon, 11, 16, 94–96
Tea cake, spiced,
Thyme, 11, 12, 13, 16, 97–101
  stuffing for poultry, 101
Thymus. *See* Thyme
Tisanes. *See* Herbal teas
Tomato, anchovy and oregano (pizza)
  pie, 72
Tomatoes, and oregano, 72
  baked, with basil, 34
Tripe, fried, with winter savory, 88

Veal chops, baked with herbs, 51
Verbena, lemon-scented, 12
Vinegar, basil, 33
  lavender, 62
  tarragon, 95
Violets, 12

Wallflowers, 12
Welsh rarebit with sage, 86
Wheel herb-gardens, 6
Wormwood, 95